Creative Collage for Crafters

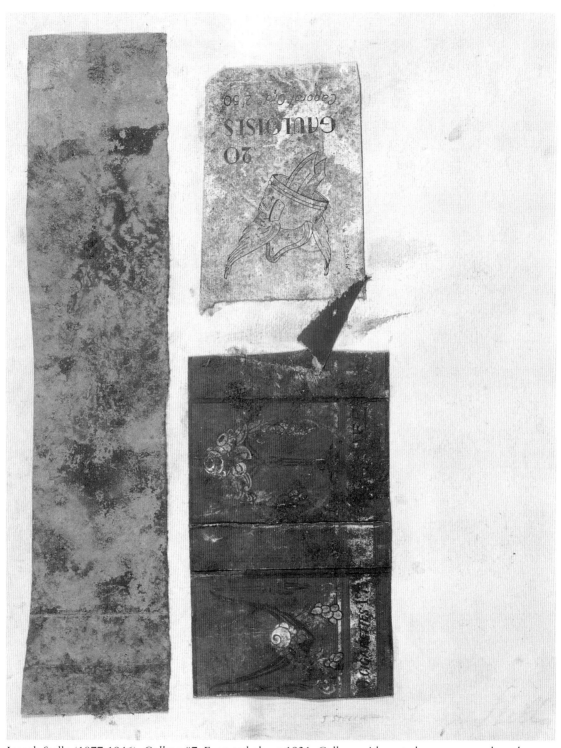

Joseph Stella (1877-1946), *Collage #7*, Executed about 1921, Collage with pasted papers on carboard, 10 x 7¾ in. (25.4 x 19.5 cm), Signed twice at lower right: J. STELLA Joseph Stella, Collection of Richard York Gallery: New York, New York

Creative Collage for Crafters

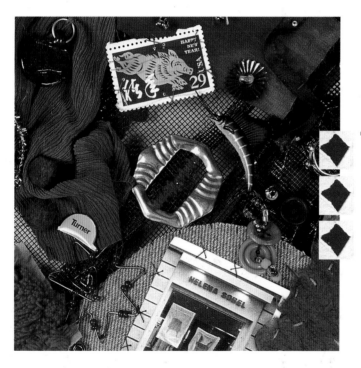

◆ Techniques
◆ Projects
◆ Inspirations

Katherine Duncan Aimone

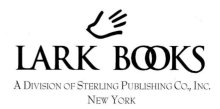

LARK BOOKS

A DIVISION OF STERLING PUBLISHING CO., INC.
NEW YORK

Dedication

This book is dedicated to my dear friend, Jackie Randel Montgomery,
who passed away in February of the year 2000. I think of you often.

Acknowledgements

Thanks to all of you—designers, artists, gallery owners, and others—who assisted
in the process of filling this book with information and stunning visuals.
Thanks to art director Celia Naranjo for a beautiful and easy-to-understand layout.
Thanks to Evan Bracken for thoughtful photography.
A special thanks goes to Michael Rosenfeld Gallery in New York for the
contribution of collage images by female artists from the early to mid-20th century.
Thanks also to Joan T. Washburn Gallery and Richard York Gallery in New York
for the contribution of historical images.

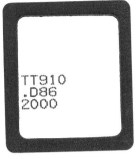

Art Direction and Production: **Celia Naranjo**
Photography: **Evan Bracken**
Editorial Assistance: **Heather Smith, Veronika Gunter**
Production Assistance: **Hannes Charen**

Library of Congress Cataloging-in-Publication Data

Duncan-Aimone, Katherine.
    Creative collage for crafters : techniques, projects, inspiratons /
    Katherine Duncan-Aimone.
       p. cm.
    Includes index.
    ISBN 1-57990-158-1
    1. collage. I. Title.

TT910.D86 2000
702'.81'2--dc21   00-041220

10 9 8 7 6 5 4 3 2 1

Published by Lark Books, a division of
Sterling Publishing Co., Inc.
387 Park Avenue South, New York, N.Y. 10016

© 2000 by Lark Books

Distributed in Canada by Sterling Publishing,
c/o Canadian Manda Group, One Atlantic Ave., Suite 105
Toronto, Ontario, Canada M6K 3E7

Distributed in Australia by Capricorn Link (Australia) Pty Ltd., P.O. Box
6651, Baulkham Hills, Business Centre
NSW 2153, Australia

If you have questions or comments about this book, please contact:
Lark Books
50 College St.
Asheville, NC 28801
(828) 253-0467

Manufactured in Hong Kong by Dai Nippon Printing Co., Ltd.

ISBN 1-57990-158-1

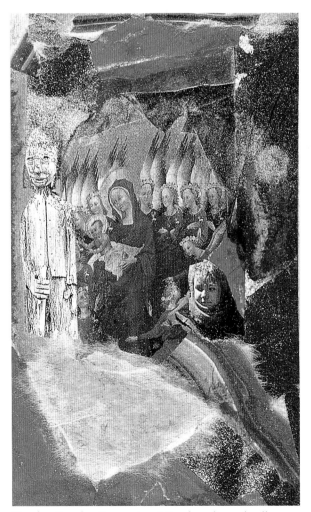

Carolyn Brooks, *Procession*, Mixed media and collage,
5 x 3 in. (12.7 x 7.6 cm)

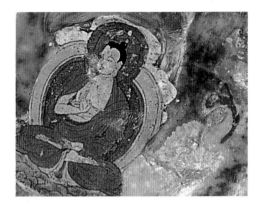

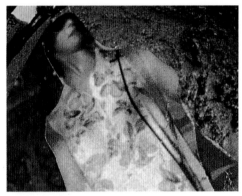

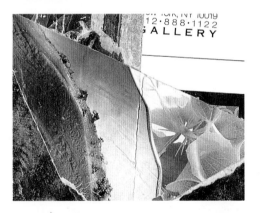

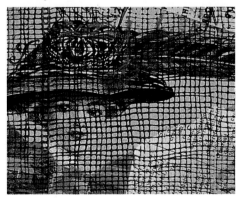

Contents

Introduction

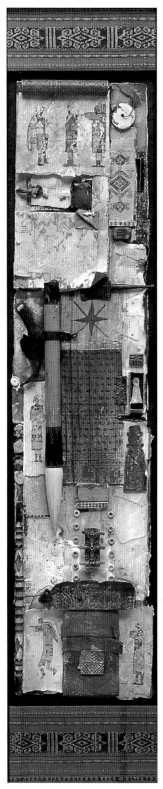

During the course of our daily lives, we're bombarded with information, images, and ideas from a great number of sources. This process can be both stimulating and overwhelming. In an effort to make some sense of chaos, we've learned to quickly sort through this barrage of stimuli—discarding what doesn't interest us and retaining what does.

Making a collage can be thought of as an extension of this process. It provides a way of creating a new meaning out of disparate images and materials. It allows those of us who love to collect things with an outlet for our obsessive tendencies. After all, gathering the materials is usually half of the process of making collage.

Collage is an accessible bridge between art and craft for those of us who think—because of some experience that influenced us early on—that we aren't artists and have no hope of becoming artists. *Anyone* can make a collage and begin to experience those indefinable moments when things "click"— when the outside world vanishes and the moment of making takes over.

The definition of the word collage (originally from the French word *coller* which means to stick) has become so broad today that it encompasses any material that can be attached to a surface. Paper is most often associated with collage because it was used by early 20th-century artists, such as Pablo Picasso and Georges Braque who brought it to history's attention. If Picasso, a constant experimenter and rebel, had had access to the wealth of materials available today, there's no doubt he would have incorporated more of them into his paintings and collages.

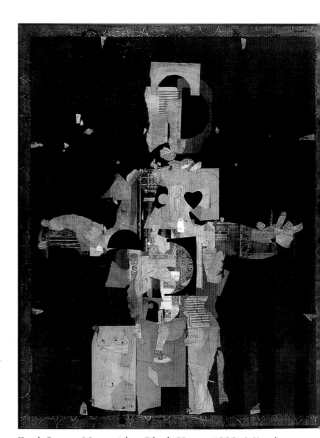

JoAnne Williams, *Artist's Diary*, 1999, Handmade embossed papers painted with oil, acrylic, watercolors, pencil, and oil crayons; Japanese brush; gold dust spoon and box from Africa; Indonesian bone calendar; African 'gris gris' (leather amulet), kimono tie, Timor lime container, bamboo, South Pacific arrowhead, 15 x 48 x 3½ in. (38.1 x 121.92 x 8.9 cm)

Fred Otnes, *Man with a Black Heart*, 1998, Mixed-media collage, 56¼ x 44¼ in. (142.9 x 112.4 cm)

Collage is an extremely personal medium. Images, words, materials, and objects that hold meaning for the individual can be incorporated into a whole that provides a vehicle for expressing anger, joy, humor, or sorrow. On the other hand, many people engage in collage solely for the sake of transforming a blank surface into a compelling one. Collage can be as simple or complex as you want it to be. It is an unlimited, forgiving, and inclusive medium without boundaries or rules.

This book was put together to encourage and celebrate the possibilities of collage for everyone—from those of us who made a decoupaged pocketbook in high school as our last shot at creative work, to those of us who express ourselves through art every day. Simple, illustrated exercises in paper, fabric, and mixed media by professional collage instructors will relieve you of any intimidating thoughts that might be lurking in your mind. Once you start looking and reading, you'll be so taken with how simple the process is, that you may find yourself filling your dining room table with accumulations of assorted materials which lead to making collages.

All the technical information that you need (and more) to make the process hassle-free is included. New, nontoxic ways to adhere materials and transfer photos are discussed, along with other information that you're not likely to come across anywhere else.

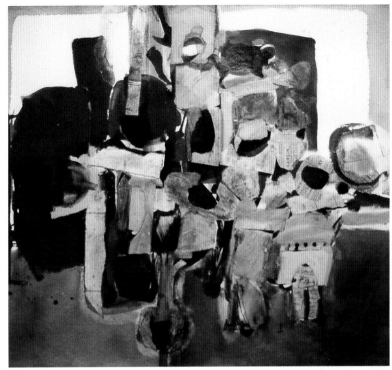

Nancy Grossman, *Cubist Club at St. Mark's*, 1963, Collage on paper, 20¼ x 22¼ in. (51.4 x 56.5 cm). Signed and dated. Courtesy of Michael Rosenfeld Gallery: New York, New York.

Most important, you'll learn how to compose your collage, whether you're approach is purely improvisational or thoroughly planned. You'll gain a sense of the breadth and excitement of collage by looking at works by professional artists. It's through this process that you'll learn the most about collage before you begin experimenting with it.

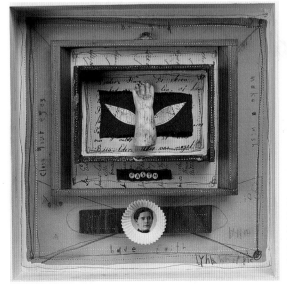

Lynn Whipple, *Faith*, 2000, mixed media collage with found objects; pencil and acrylic on wood, 12 x 12 x 12 in. (30.5 x 30.5 x 30.5 cm)

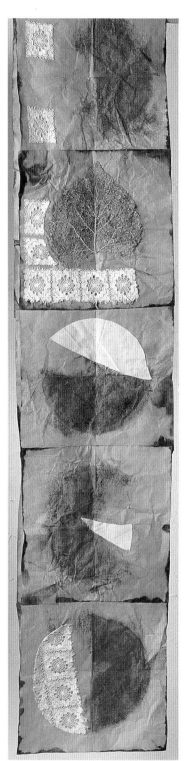

A collage can be done successfully on any blank surface. In addition to putting it on canvas, board, or paper, a collage can become a part of your everyday life in the form of a tabletop, collaged book, or even a wastebasket. Numerous examples of this idea created by talented designers and artists fill the pages of this book.

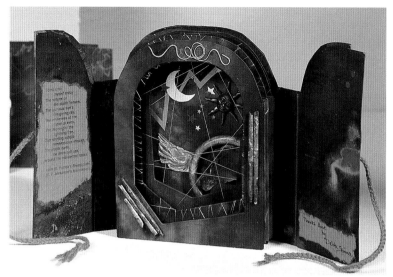

Delda Skinner, *St. Patrick's Breastplate*, 1999, Tunnel book collaged with painted handmade paper, old magazine copy, hammered wire, thread, yarn, handwritten poem, and jewelry

You'll see a collaged lunchbox created by a painter, a coat rack embellished with collaged metal by a weaver, and an unusual altar dreamed up by an art therapist. Ideas that range from clever to profound are brought to life on a variety of unexpected forms. We hope that these creative pieces will open your mind to the limitless possibilities of collage, and lead you to engage in your own satisfying creations.

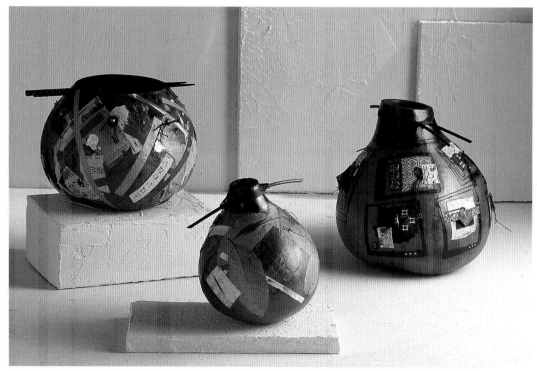

Jean Penland, *Untitled*, 2000, Collaged hanging screen composed of unbleached coffee filters soaked with grounds, leaf skeleton, lace, and cotton duck canvas

Diane Peterson, *Untitled*, 2000, Collaged and woodburned gourds with assorted papers, dried leaves, tea bags, gold leaf, coins, brass nails, and chopsticks

Collage in the Past and the Present

THE ACT OF CUTTING AND PASTING materials together to create an interesting surface was done long before it was called "collage". Japanese landscapes well over a thousand years old combine cutout papers, and the Victorians garnished their valentines with bits of paper and lace. Variations of collage happen in every culture. The introduction of collage as an art form is credited to Pablo Picasso (1881-1973) and Georges Braque (1882-1963), who began making collages in the early 20th century from newspaper clippings, colored papers, tobacco wrappings, and wallpapers. Collage was a vehicle through which these artists could explore, in an unencumbered fashion, their developing ideas about Cubism. Rather than creating the illusion of a three-dimensional scene on a two-dimensional surface, as most art since the Renaissance had done, Cubist artists sought to portray objects simultaneously on several planes. By abstracting from nature, they gradually eliminated the imitation of reality in their paintings and collages.

During this same period of art history, the well-known French artist Henri Matisse (1869-1954) also added collage to his repertoire of painting and sculpture. His work in collage culminated in large-scale designs composed of colored paper designs created between 1949 and 1951 for the chapel St. Marie du Rosaire in Vence, near Nice, France. During his later years, collage allowed the sight-impaired Matisse to create simple but powerful abstractions distilled from his earlier explorations of color and design.

The effectiveness of the fabric and paper collages of American poet and painter Anne Ryan (1889-1954) has been compared to that of Matisse's later collages. A 1948 exhibition of collage works by German artist Kurt Schwitters (1887-1948) inspired her to begin making collages at age 59. Her delicate, cerebral works in this medium engage a few simple elements in a provocative manner.

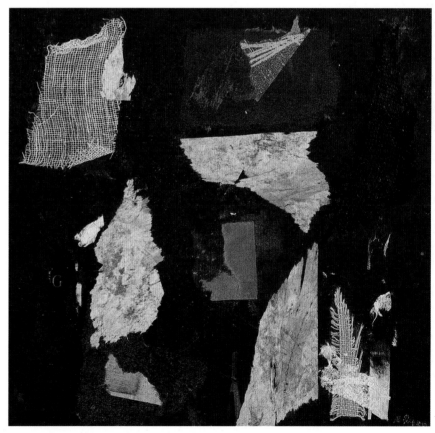

Anne Ryan, *Untitled (#395-A)*, c. 1949, Collage, 6⅞ x 7⅛ in. (17.6 x 18.5 cm), Signed lower right and verso, Courtesy of Joan T. Washburn Gallery: New York, New York

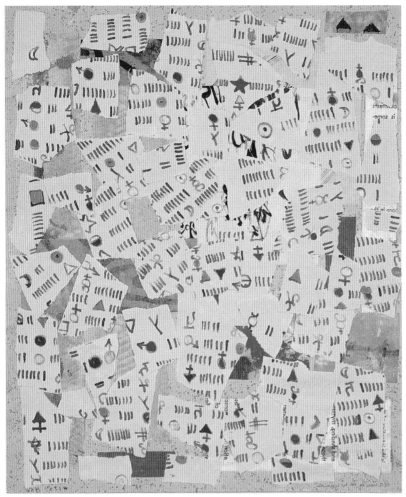

Other early 20th century artists continued the exploration of abstract art through collage. American sculptor Gertrude Greene (1904-1956) lived in Paris during the late 1920s and early 1930s where she was influenced by Cubism and Constructivism. Constructivism is often thought of as beginning when Picasso created a sheet-metal-and-wire construction of a guitar in 1912 that translated the angular forms of his collages into three dimensions. During this same period of time, Russian Constructivists created large-scale sculptural works that reflected the technological society in which they were created. These abstract pieces were devoid of references to the naturalistic world.

Through her own artistic vision permeated with this environment of ideas, Gertrude Greene's work became more and more abstract as she pressed toward her own version of geometric purity. She used paper collages to informally explore her ideas of form and space that would later be translated into wood reliefs.

Fiber artist Eve Peri (1897-1966) grew up in an American home where her women

Charmion von Wiegand, *Palimpset*, 1956, Oil and collage on paper, 13¼ x 11½ in. (33.6 x 29.2 cm), Signed, Courtesy of Michael Rosenfeld Gallery: New York, New York

Bottom right: Gertrude Greene, Untitled, 1934, Paper collage, 6½ x 10½ in. (16.5 x 26.7 cm), Signed, Courtesy of Michael Rosenfeld Gallery: New York, New York

Charmion von Wiegand (1896-1983), an American painter who was a follower and supporter of Dutch painter Piet Mondrian (1872-1944), helped to organize the first show of Schwitters's work in America. The influence of both Mondrian and Schwitters led her to pursue abstract, idealistic collages filled with personal symbols.

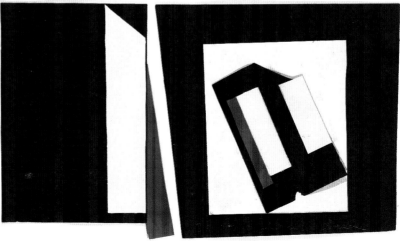

relatives were constantly sewing, embroidering, and stitching cloth. Peri first saw the paintings of Matisse around 1930, which led her to pursue a career as an artist. She combined her interest in art

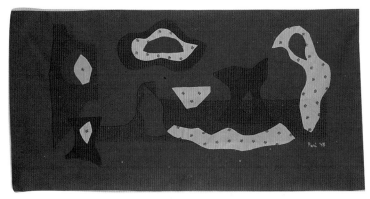

with her love of embroidery, appliqué, and textiles. A one-woman exhibition of her work in 1948 at the Philadelphia Art Alliance introduced works such as the fiber collage entitled *Luan Moresca* (1948). The influence of Matisse is apparent in the simple forms and vibrant colors of this piece.

As a movement, fiber art came into it's own during the 1960s and 70s. Lenore

Tawney (b. 1907) helped to elevate the status of fiber art through her use of fiber as sculpture. In 1964, she began making collages from objects that she had collected in her studio. Her collage works, which often contain printed words positioned like woven strips, harken back to a period of her life when she supported herself as a proofreader.

Today, collage is used by many contemporary artists as an addition to multi-media works. Well-known artists such as Jasper Johns (b. 1930), Miriam Schapiro (b. 1923), Robert Rauschenberg (b. 1925), Larry Rivers (b.1923), and Betye Saar (b. 1926) have exploited the medium for their purposes. Over the past century, collage has been added to the vocabulary of art as a rich source of imagery, content, and design for artists.

Top left: Eve Peri, *Luna Maresca*, 1945-46, Fabric collage, 16¾ x 33½ in. (42.5 x 85.9 cm), Signed, Courtesy of Michael Rosenfeld Gallery: New York, New York

Bottom left: Betye Saar, *Mother and Children in Blue*, 1998, Mixed-media collage on paper, 8⅝ x 6½ in. (21.9 x 16.5 cm), Collection of Whitney Museum of American Art, Purchased with funds from the Drawing Committee (00.46)

Bottom right: Lenore Tawney, *Untitled*, 1983, Paper collage, 5¾ x 5¼ in. (14.6 x 13.2 cm), Signed, Courtesy of Michael Rosenfeld Gallery: New York, New York

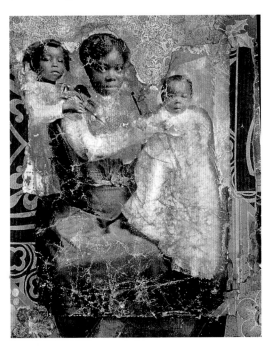

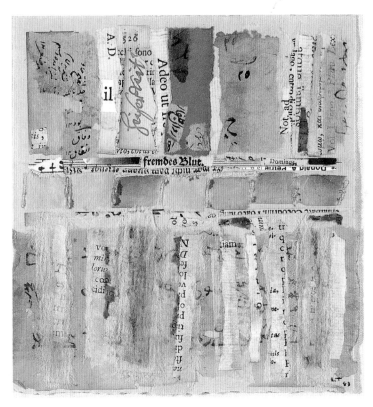

Hunting & Gathering

SOME OF US NEED NO EXCUSE to rummage through thrift stores, scavenge through urban trashbins, or stick our noses into attic boxes. Nevertheless, if you need justification for indulging in a natural human instinct, then collage may give you just the excuse you've been looking for. You'll have carte blanche to be obsessive.

collage, you'll probably have the opposite problem—you may end up with more ideas than you can use!

The process of hunting and gathering materials can be half of the process of making a finished collage piece. There are any number of ways to approach this stage of your work.

The choices that you make at this stage determine much of the makeup of the finished piece. Finding a particular paper, fabric, or unusual material can easily lead you to the nucleus of an idea. If you don't have

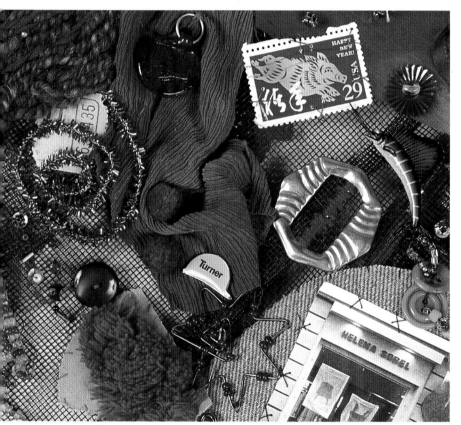

Mary D'Alton, Collaged vest (detail of project on page 98), 2000.

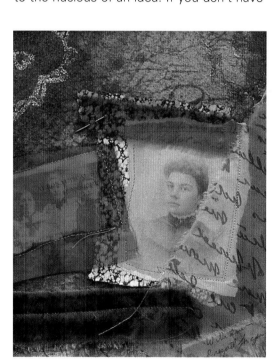

Niki Bonnett, *Correspondence I*, 1999, Dyed fabric, dye-painted fabric, resist-dyed fabric, hot foil stamped fabric, solvent transfers, color photocopies, black and white photocopies on silk organza. Machine appliqued and quilted. 17 x 14 in. (43.2 x 35.6 cm)

Lots of books will tell you how to come up with ideas for making art by leading you by the hand and encouraging you with exercises that will keep you from "running out of ideas." If you take up the medium of

a clue as to what you want to make, begin by collecting materials that interest you for any number of reasons: their sheer beauty, color, or texture; their personal significance; or their need (in your mind) to be preserved. You can decide exactly how you're going to use them later.

Open your eyes to the world of possibilities, and you'll begin to see potential collage components everywhere—movie tickets, postcards, exhibition catalogs, matchbooks, paper, colored tissue papers, gift wraps, stamps, wallpaper samples, magazine and newspaper cutouts, photos, sheet music, maps, sketches, cardboard, fabric, felt, leather, string, metal scraps, buttons, dried natural materials, window screen, and small found objects.

Once you've gathered materials, you may find that you want to choose a theme, or the composition of the materials themselves may become the theme. If you're working with photos, for instance, it is natural to be drawn to a theme since you're using recognizable subject matter. If you love golf, for instance, you might pursue a collection of golf photos taken on vacations. If you are dazzled by color and texture, you'll need no more of an excuse to gather up luscious papers, fabrics, and other potential surface additions than the fact that they'll make intriguing compositional elements. There are no rules for all of this—don't try to make scavenging into a science, or you'll spoil the fun.

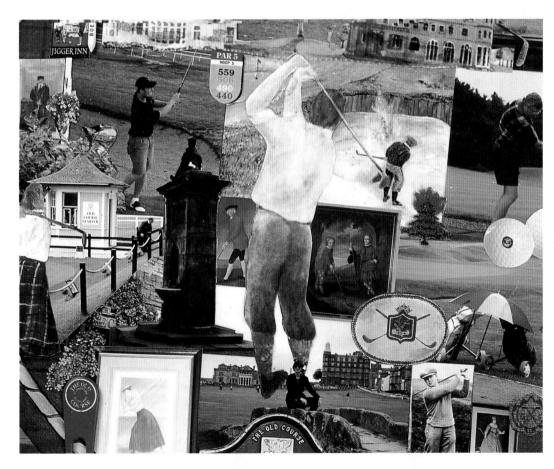

Tana Boerger, Collaged tabletop (detail of project on page 66), 2000.

Creating an Environment for Your Work

Don't take yourself too seriously. And don't be too serious about not taking yourself too serious.

—Howard Ogden

IF YOU DON'T HAVE AN OFFICIAL STUDIO in your home, you can set up a work area in a spare room or dining room that will serve you well. Take the time to organize this area, and you'll spend more time being creative and less digging through boxes for a lost piece of paper or a misplaced bottle of glue. As much as it may offend your carefree nature, a few simple plastic drawers or shoe boxes can transport you into a new realm of organization. Separate your collections of papers, fabrics, and other materials in a way that makes sense for you.

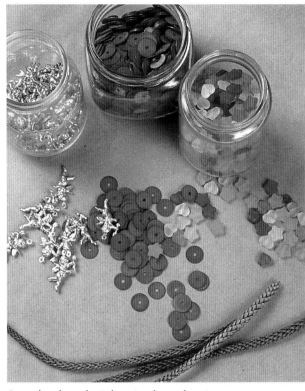

Store beads and trinkets in clean glass jars.

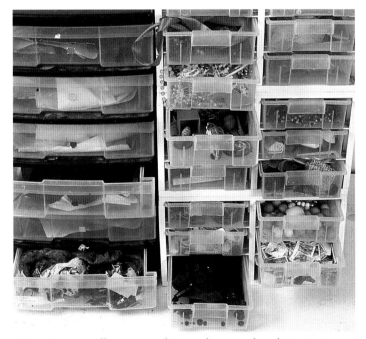

Separate your collage materials according to color, shape, texture, or any category that makes sense to you.

Then divide adhesives, paints, pencils, markers, and other supplies into categories. Keep your cutting tools, such as scissors and mat knives, in a drawer or box. Label each container, and take time to put the stuff back when you're finished. If you're working in a room that has other purposes, keep your supplies in a corner or put them on a shelf when you're not working.

Find an organizational system that works for you, and create a visual environment that stimulates you. Use masking tape to fill your walls with cutout pictures of artwork that you like, or tape up some of your choice compositions or sketches.

Cover your work surface with some sort of absorbent, thick paper, such as newsprint, kraft paper, or paper grocery bags that you've taped together. Then you can whisk the paper away after you've finished a session of work. (By the way, after you've dripped too much paint and glue all over the paper, it can be cut into pieces that make great additions to a collage.)

And, finally, take time for the most important part of doing creative work. Put your mind in the mood by allowing yourself to slow down before you begin. Put on comfortable clothes. Pet your cat. Hit the play button and listen to your favorite composer. Thumb through a book of work by an admired artist that inspires you.

If you're really not in the mood to work, but you know that you really want to, you may get your creative juices flowing by making some very simple collages. In a totally non-serious manner, play with colors, textures, and shapes by ripping, cutting, and juxtaposing papers and other materials. Make marks with pencils, paints, or whatever you have on hand.

Whatever you do, don't approach your work with preconceived notions of becoming the next undiscoverd Picasso, making a fortune off of selling your work, or even winning a ribbon at the county fair. You'll most likely end up with a stiff, self-conscious composition that won't win any prizes anyway. And you'll miss out on all the good stuff that happens when you relax. So suspend judgment of yourself, get in there with your bare hands and imagination, and enjoy!

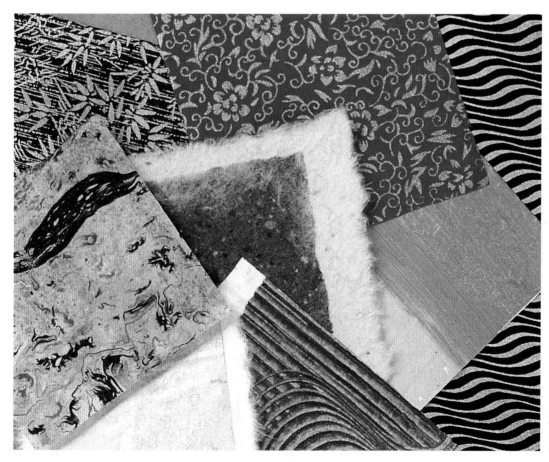

Spread out a selection of papers that you've collected to get ideas going.

In the following demonstrations, artist Jonathan Talbot combines the simplest of materials cut into three shapes to create thematic collages.

Creating Collage Compositions with a Few Simple Elements

Assemble papers and cutting instruments of your choice (scissors, mat knife, or hole puncher), and see if you can create your own themed collage with only three elements.

Moby Dick Collage

1. Assemble three sheets of paper or other material that you want to use for your collage. Cut or tear them into pieces with tools of your choice (photo 1).

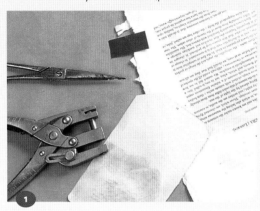

2. Create representative shapes (such as the whale) through tearing or cutting. Arrange the pieces on your substrate (photo 2). Attach the pieces with an adhesive of your choice (see pages 20 through 24).

Paper Moon Collage

1. Assemble three sheets of paper or other material that you want to use for your collage. Use a mat knife to cut out shapes from one of the pieces to create a silhouetted image (such as the trees that you see here [photo 1]).

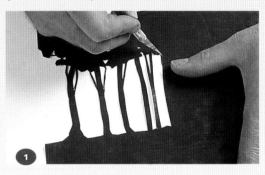

2. Cut out the other components that will make up your collage (photo 2).

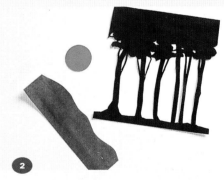

3. Layer the pieces to form a collaged image (photo 3). Attach the pieces with an adhesive (see pages 20 through 24).

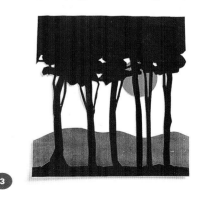

Materials & Tools

PAPER

Paper is the most commonly used component of collage. It's readily available to anyone, it's inexpensive, and it's so overwhelmingly prevalent on the planet today that we throw out tons of it every day. You need look no further than the print media that's otherwise destined for your trashcan for potential collage sources—newspapers, magazines, letters, and junk mail.

Collage gives you a wonderful opportunity to relieve yourself of a lot of guilt. Not only can you incorporate the unique and beautiful wrapping paper that your husband so carefully chose for you into something lasting, but you can help (in a small way) to teach your children about the value of recycling. Papers of any sort, even if mundane at first glance, can be transformed by cutting or tearing them into shapes, adding color to them, and arranging them into a composition with other materials.

Whatever you do, pick out papers that you like, and experiment with them to see how they behave when they're glued down and combined. If you're characteristically a planner, you may enjoy collecting papers in various colors and separating them into boxes so that you can select from them while you're working. If you're more improvisational by nature, you may prefer to collect a diverse group of papers and combine unlikely colors and textures in an unplanned manner.

From fine handmade Japanese papers to throwaway print media, your choices are unlimited. Visit craft stores, art supply stores, and stationery stores to get an overview of how many choices are available to you among purchased papers.

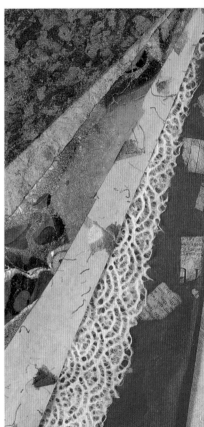

Beautiful textured papers can be purchased.

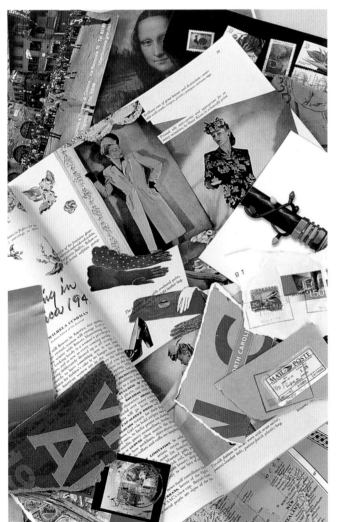

Found papers from many sources can be used for collage.

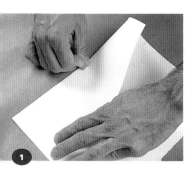

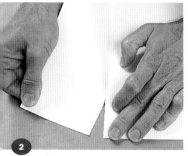

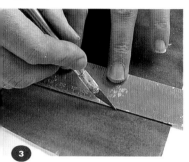

For example, semitranslucent papers, such as tissue paper, are perfect for layering and veiling the images on opaque papers.

Combine both torn and cut paper edges in your compositions to create contrasts. By tearing paper, you'll create soft edges. Thinner papers tear more easily, and you'll find they tear more predictably along the grain.

To create a straight line, tear paper along a folded crease (photos 1 and 2), or along the edge of a metal ruler. Cut paper with sharp scissors to create crisp edges. Use a mat knife to make clean, straight cuts along the edge of a metal ruler (photo 3). To cut thick paper, use a mat knife fitted with a thick blade, and for thin paper, use a knife with a narrow, fine blade. Replace the blades frequently so that they don't catch on the paper and rip it. Invest in a cutting mat to prolong the life of your blade.

PHOTOGRAPHS

Photographs from print media as well as personal photographs have always been a primary source for collage pieces, allowing the artist to add images that affect the piece's content. Many collage artists juxtapose seemingly unrelated photographs to create new meanings. The use of photographs in this manner is also known as *photomontage.*

Photographs can be used in their original state or altered on a photocopier. They can be enlarged or reduced, lightened or darkened, or copied onto colored paper. The possibilities are unlimited for changing them into components that fit the collage you plan to create. Several photographs can be copied at once and cut into pieces that are copied again to abstract and change the images with which you're working. You may also find it interesting to copy photos in several sizes and repeat the image in your collage. Photo transfers make interesting additions to a collage. A transfer process that works well for collage is described on the following pages.

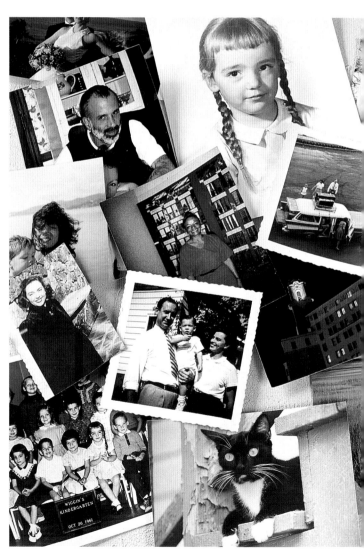

Personal photographs can be added to a collage in their original state or altered on a photocopier.

Photo Transfers

There are many ways to transfer photographic images to paper. The following method works extremely well for collage. It leaves the image standing on the receiving surface without a trace of the paper that originally held it. Artist Jonathan Talbot demonstrates it in the following steps. He notes that this method has been passed down from one artist to another.

To transfer images with this method, you'll need a sheet of "image transfer paper" (clay-coated unvarnished paper that is often used for the inside pages of magazines [see page 112 for supplier, or ask a local printer if you can purchase some from them]), an image to photocopy onto the image transfer paper, acrylic gloss medium, a paintbrush, a tacking iron (preferably with an adjustable temperature gauge), a sheet of release paper (reusable silicon-coated paper which will not stick to anything [see page 112 for supplier] and a woven cotton cloth [such as a scrap of old bedsheet].)

1. Photocopy your image onto the slick side of the image transfer paper. Cover the face of the image with acrylic gloss medium (photo 1). Allow it to dry. (Do not cover the back of the image transfer paper.)

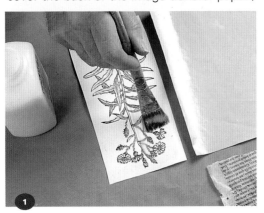

2. Coat the surface which is to receive the image with acrylic gloss medium (photo 2). Allow it to dry.

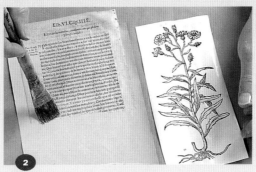

3. Place the image facedown on the receiving surface (photo 3).

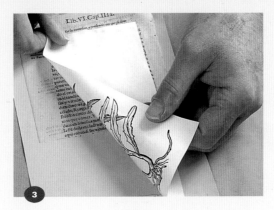

4. Place a piece of release paper on top of these two sheets large enough to protect the collage from the iron (photo 4). Heat the tacking iron to a temperature of around 200° F (158° C), and iron the transfer into place.

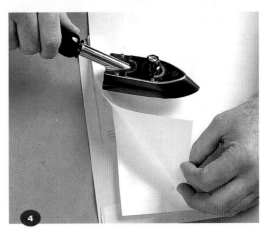

Artist Jonathan Talbot demonstrates a method of photo transfer that works well with collage.

(continued on page 20)

Photo Transfers, continued

5. Wrap the cotton cloth around your fingertip, dip it in water to wet thoroughly, and use it to gently scrub the back of the transfer until bits of paper begin to roll up (photo 5). Continue the process of rubbing to magically reveal the image (photo 6).

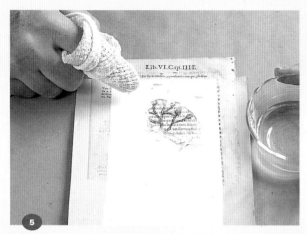

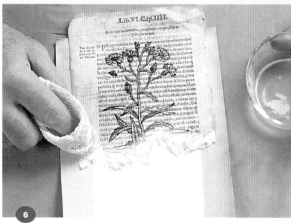

Note: Images that are transferred with this method will be reversed. If it is important to retain the original orientation of the image, photocopy the image onto transparent film, flip the film over so that the image is facing up on the photocopy machine, and then recopy it onto the transfer paper.

ADHESIVES

Experiment with adhesives to see which works best for the papers or other materials you plan to use. White craft glue (PVA glue) works fine for most papers, and it is acid-free and non-toxic. To apply this glue fluidly, water it down slightly with water, and paint it onto the area where you plan to place the paper. Press the paper into place on top of the glue, smooth out any air bubbles with your fingers or a brayer (a narrow wallpaper smoother works well), and allow it to dry. As the collage dries, the paper may warp slightly from the wetness of the glue. Continue to smooth it out if this happens, but don't worry if

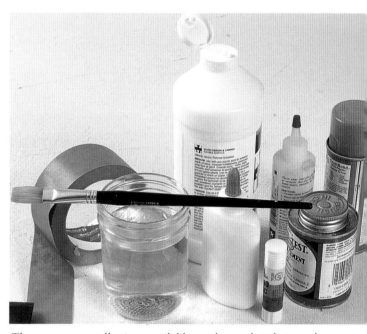

There are many adhesives available on the market that can be used for collage—from simple white glue to rubber cement.

you end up with some wrinkles that add texture to your collage. After the collage dries, you can paint a coat of glue on top of your collage to seal it. Even though it will look milky when you apply the glue, it will dry clear and hard.

Acrylic medium (acrylic polymer emulsion), which is used by artists to dilute acrylic paint, makes a wonderful, acid-free adhesive for collage. This product is

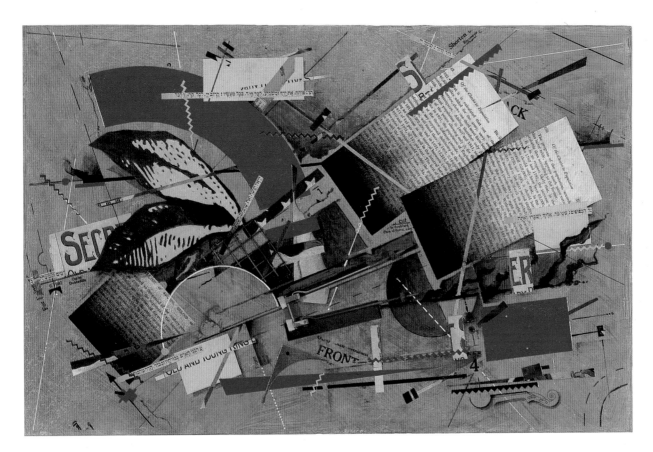

available in liquid or gel form, as well as mat or gloss finish. Because acrylic medium is the stuff that suspends pigment to make acrylic paint, it behaves like a clear paint. Many artists like the fact that textured brush strokes show on the surface to which acrylic medium is applied, lending the collage a more painterly look. Acrylic medium is a natural to use if you're planning to add acrylic paint to the collage.

Before you begin working, you can paint a coat of it on your surface to serve as a primer or sealer. To use it as a glue, squeeze it out into a cup, and paint it onto the surface with a brush as you would white glue. Water it down if you want a thinner consistency. Apply papers, fabrics, or other components, and press them down with your fingers, a brayer, or your paintbrush. Add another layer of medium

on top of the collage if you'd like to seal it with a varnish-like finish.

Glue sticks are handy for adhering small, intricate collages. Epoxy resins, made up of one part adhesive, one part hardener/catalyst, are commonly used for attaching heavier objects to a collage. Rubber cement works well for applying delicate papers without any worries about the glue soaking and wrinkling the surface. Pieces can also be moved around and reaffixed if needed. Aerosol glues work well for this same purpose, but must be used with caution because they can be hazardous to breathe. Artist Jonathan Talbot has developed a non-toxic method for applying both papers and fabric without liquid adhesives and without wrinkling that is described on the following pages.

Jonathan Talbot, *Jam Session*, 1992, Collage of painted and found papers, paint, ink, string, metal, and wood on museum board mounted on watercolor paper, Image: 15½ x 24 in. (39.4 x 61 cm), Paper: 22 x 30 in. (55.9 x 76.2 cm)

Creating a Collage Without Liquid Adhesives

Collage artist Jonathan Talbot discovered, somewhat by accident, a non-toxic technique for adhering collage elements to a surface without the use of liquid adhesives. Sound like magic? The first time you try this, you'll probably think it is, even though this method is accomplished with simple materials. This technique works with paper, fabric, foil, string, and other materials.

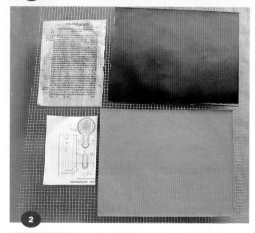

This method allows you to arrange and rearrange a composition on your surface (often in layers) without having to remove elements when you're ready to attach them. By doing this, you won't lose any of the placement of your components. This method also eliminates wrinkling and drying time.

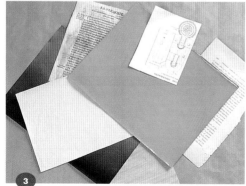

In order to undertake this method, you'll need a bottle of acrylic gloss medium, a wide paintbrush, clean paper, some double-sided sheets of release paper (paper coated with silicone that doesn't stick to your collage [see page 112 for source]), a tacking iron (preferably one with a variable temperature

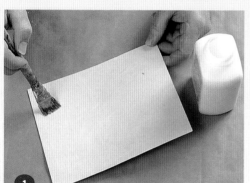

control), and cutting tools such as scissors, a mat knife, or hole punches. For the purpose of drying pieces of paper, you can use a piece of chicken wire or other metal wire to serve as a drying rack.

1. Use the paintbrush to coat the substrate to which you plan to apply the collage with a coat of acrylic medium (photo 1). (If you want to create a neutral ground for your collage, first paint the substrate with a coat of acrylic paint before adding the acrylic medium.)

2. Assemble the papers and other collage materials that you plan to use to make your collage. Lay them out on clean sheets of paper, and use your paintbrush to coat the face of each with an even coat of acrylic gloss medium (gloss works better than mat). Remove the materials before they begin to dry, and place them on a sheet of chicken wire or other metal wire placed on your work surface (photo 2). After the medium has dried on the front of the materials, coat the backs of them, place them facedown on the rack, and allow them to dry. Your materials are now ready to use (photo 3).

3. Prepare your precoated materials for assembling by cutting or tearing them into pieces. You can use a variety of tools to create different edges: a hole punch (photo 4), plain or pattern-edged scissors (photo 5), or a mat knife (photo 6). You can also tear papers into smaller pieces (photo 7).

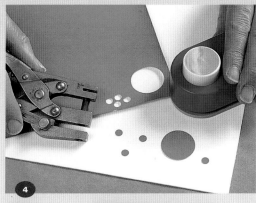

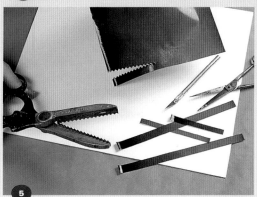

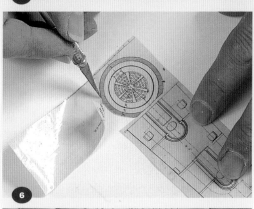

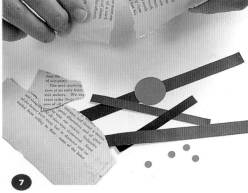

4. When you're satisfied with the pieces you've cut or torn, place them on the substrate (photo 8). Play with the arrangement until you strike a combination that you like (photo 9 and 10). (During this process, subtract pieces if you need to, or cut new pieces that you want to add from your pre-coated materials.)

5. If your tacking iron has a variable temperature control, heat it to 225° F (107° C) to begin with. (You may need to adjust this

(continued on page 24)

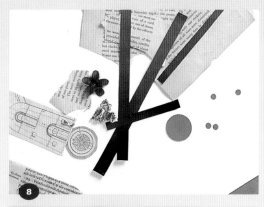

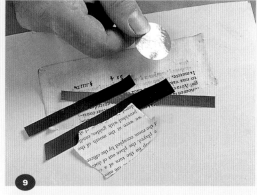

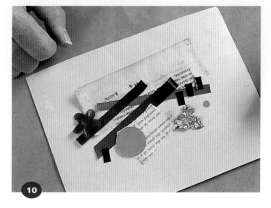

Collage Without Liquid Adhesives,
(continued)

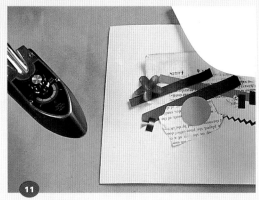

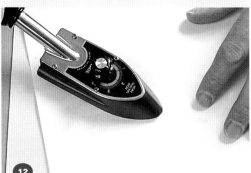

to a higher temperature if you are using thick materials, or a lower temperature if you're using thin ones. Experiment to find the right setting for your materials.) Hold the iron in your hand, and use your other hand to place a sheet of release paper on top of the assembled collage (photo 11). Use the iron to burnish, or rub, the surface of the release paper with an even pressure and at a consistent pace until you've adhered all areas of the collage (photo 12). (The heat will fuse the acrylic medium that has been applied to all the surfaces.)

6. Remove the release paper to reveal your neatly adhered collage (photo 13).

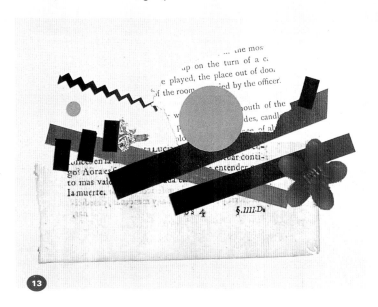

FABRIC

If you've ever spent a portion of your time sewing, you know the joys of "collecting" fabrics (the ones that are piled up under your bed along with your good intentions). Fabric collage, based for a great part on the quilting tradition, is extremely popular today.

Fabrics can be used alone to make a collage, or combined with other materials. Scraps are a natural. Use a pair of good fabric scissors to cut your fabric into smaller pieces for collage. Save these scissors for fabric only; don't cut paper with them, or they'll become dull.

If you're adding fabric components to a paper or mixed media collage, they can be glued onto the surface. Collages made primarily of fabric are often made using a combination of gluing and some sewing to attach the pieces. Fusing pieces of cloth together with fusible web is another option.

The assembly of fabric collages are approached in many ways by artists. Often, one large piece of thick fabric is used as the

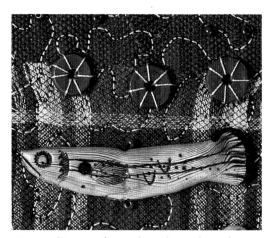

Topstitching can be used on the surface of a fabric collage to add texture to the design as well as hold pieces together.(See project on page 84.)

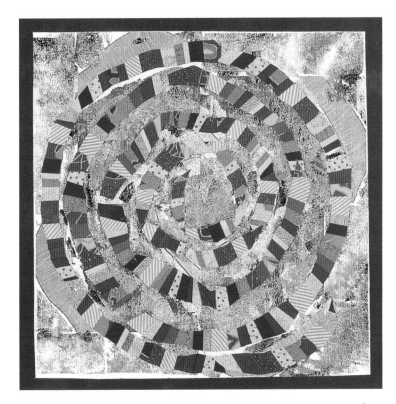

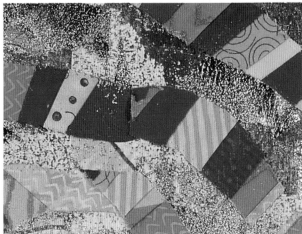

Catherine Dwore, *Labyrinth*, 1998, Collage with muslin, dye discharged fabric, pieced printed fabrics, photo transfers, metallic foil, fusible web, and thread, 27 x 27 in. (68.6 x 68.6 cm)

support for the layered fabric pieces, which are sewn on top by hand or machine. Lines of topstitching are often used to embellish the surface of the fabric collage as well as hold the pieces together. Beads, buttons, and small objects can then be sewn on top of the collaged fabric.

Other fabric collages are assembled like quilts without the batting. Piecework is done with small scraps of fabric that are assembled in an improvisational manner, resembling many traditional African-American quilts. Artist Sandra Rowland collects fabrics from every source imaginable, and combines them into quilt-like collages that develop as she makes them (see pages 27 and 28).

Fabric can also be used in collage without any sewing. After years of struggling with machine and hand sewing, textile artist Laura Breitman learned a method of

attaching collage pieces that to a ground without sewing them (see pages 22 through 24). The freedom that this method lent to her work allowed her to begin creating complex, representational images

Sandra Rowland, *Certainty*, 1998, Pieced, quilted, and beaded cotton fabric, 46½ x 32 in. (118.1 x 81.3 cm).

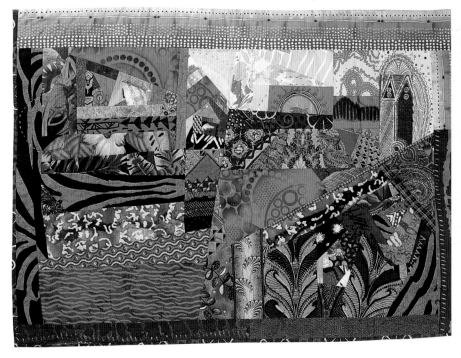

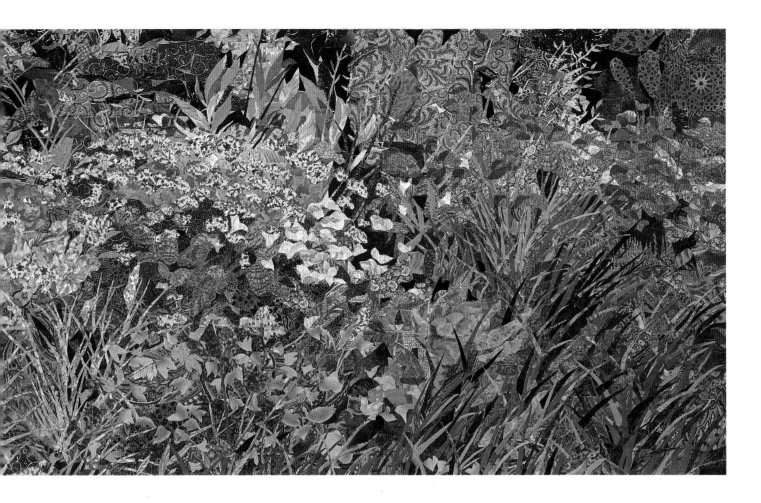

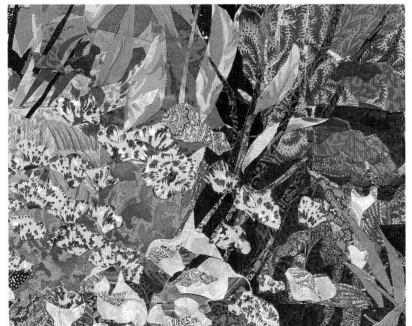

Laura Breitman, *In Full Bloom*, 1998, Fabric collage, 22 x 38 in.
(55.9 x 96.52 cm)

with fabric that she describes as "painting with fabric." She incorporates hundreds, and sometimes thousands, of fabric fragments into her collages.

If you aren't familiar with the wide range of fabrics available today, you're in for a treat. Go to a large fabric store, and enjoy the experience of touching and looking at the variety of textures, patterns, and colors. Dig through sale bins that contain small, inexpensive remnants that are perfect for collage. Use fabric in combination with other media, experiment with dyeing or painting it, or cut images from it for use in a collage as you would paper. Fabric is a varied and vibrant source of color, texture, and image for collage.

Sewing a Simple Fabric Collage

Artist Sandra Rowland demonstrates how to combine bits and pieces of fabric to create a collage.

Fabric artist Sandra Rowland loves to work improvisationally to combine bits and pieces of fabrics. Rowland's studio, stockpiled with bins of fabrics, buttons, beads, and trinkets, is an optical delight. In the following steps, she demonstrates how to use scraps of fabric to sew together a rudimentary fabric collage in the same manner that you would make a quilt. The sewn-together composite can be made into a wall piece or a bed covering.

To do this, you'll need scraps of your favorite fabrics, a rotary cutting wheel and mat, a clear plastic ruler, a threaded sewing machine, and a clothes iron.

1. Select scraps of fabric that will combine well visually (photo 1). Choose two pieces of fabric to join together, and use the rotary cutting wheel and plastic ruler to trim one of the edges of each where you plan to sew them together (photo 2).

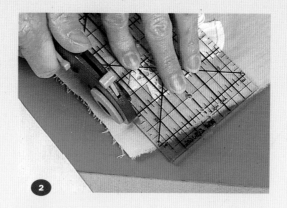

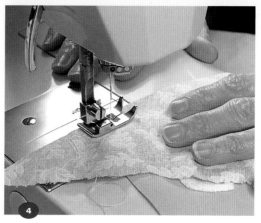

2. With the wrong sides of the fabric pieces together, line up the cut edges (photo 3). Use the sewing machine to sew together the two pieces along the joined edge with a ⅝-inch (1.6 cm) seam (photo 4). Place the piece on your work surface,

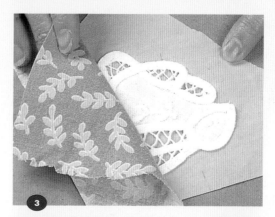

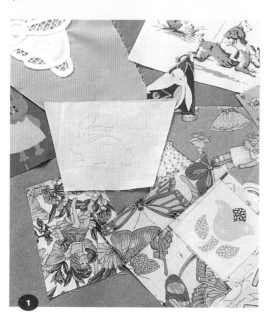

(continued on page 28)

and flip the pieces out to reveal the front of the fabric. Flatten the seam with your fingers.

3. Choose another piece of fabric to add to your piece, and sew it to another side of it as you did in steps 1 and 2. Press out your fabric composite with a heated iron to flatten it (photo 5).

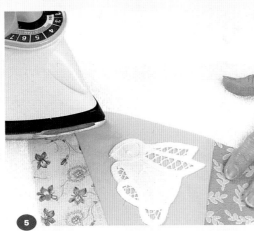

4. Use the cutting wheel to trim this piece if needed (photo 6). Continue to add pieces of fabric to create your improvisational composition.

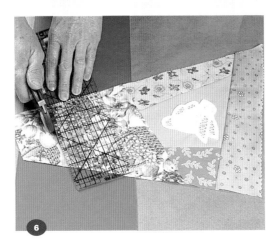

5. Create a large piece of any size that you want by combining pieces of fabric (photo 7).

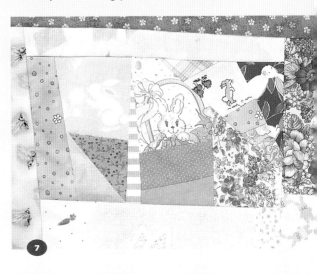

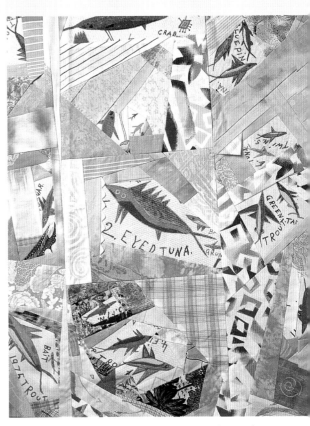

Sandra Rowland, *Carpe Diem!*, 1999, Fabric collage made from a pair of old white denim jeans that had been printed with fish. Drawing, painting, stamping, rickrack added to fabric, 63 x 96 in. (160 x 243 cm)

MIXED MEDIA

The construction of sculptural works of art made by combining non-art objects and materials is known as *assemblage*, which may be thought of as the three-dimensional counterpart of collage. Many collage artists incorporate objects into their work, blurring the definitions between collage and assemblage. Works that combine all sorts of materials and media are loosely called *mixed media*—a term which simply expresses the freedom that today's artist has to incorporate anything and everything into artwork.

Collage is a perfect outlet for mixed media interpretations. There are no rules. Anything that you can use from nature, the trash, the dump, or your collection of odds and ends may add visual interest to your composition. You can glue, sew, or screw odds and ends to your collage, depending upon the materials or objects that you're adding. For instance, mixed media artist Cori Saraceni affixes computer parts, bicycle wheels, and metals onto wood to create her collage/assemblage pieces.

Mixed media collages elevate everyday objects, both organic and man-made, into the realm of art by *recontextualizing* them (placing them in environments that endow them with new meaning). This form of collage is incredibly popular, due in part to the surplus of available materials and an interest in recycling. More important than this is the broadened definition of art embracing unlimited materials and themes which has emerged during the 20th century, and which will no doubt continue to expand during the 21st century.

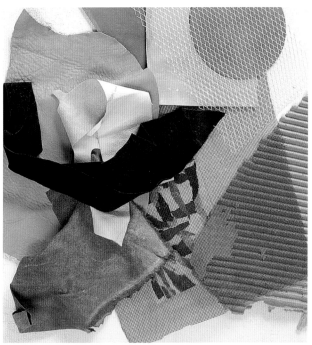

A variety of media including leather, cardboard, and metal can be used in collage.

Cori Saraceni, *Riding a Hard Drive into the New Millenium*, 1999, Stainless steel wire, bicycle wheel, viscose, acrylic paint, computer motherboards and other parts, spray paint, 36 x 38 in. (91.4 x 121.9 cm)

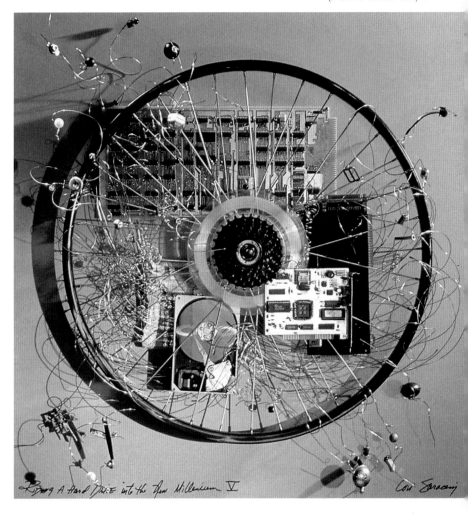

A few simple elements can be combined to create a beautiful collage.

Assembling a Simple Mixed Media Collage

Mixed media artist Pei Ling Becker uses objects, papers, and other media to create collage pieces with overtones of her Asian upbringing. She has an eye for her materials that comes naturally, and she combines them in ways that create striking compositions. In the following demonstrations, she shows how a few simple elements can be combined to make small, effective collages using paper, metal screen, rocks, and other materials. The components can be applied to heavy paper or another substrate with an adhesive of your choice (see pages 20 through 24).

Mixed Media Collage #1

1. Assemble the materials that you plan to combine into a collage, and trim papers or other flat materials with scissors or a mat knife into shapes that you plan to layer from largest to smallest (photo 1). (We used hand-dyed paper, thin metal screen, patterned paper, plain paper, a small twig, and a gold trinket.)

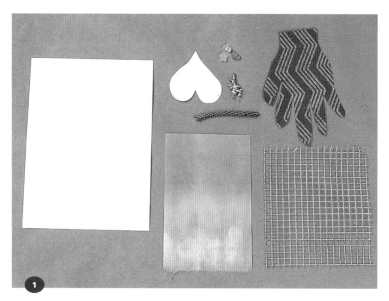

2. Layer the components so that a portion of each preceding material shows underneath the one you're adding (photos 2 through 5). Attach the pieces with an adhesive.

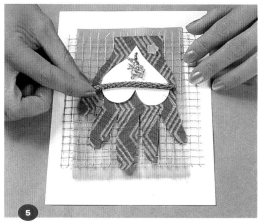

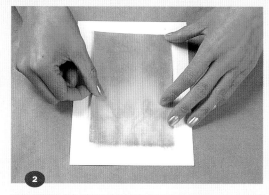

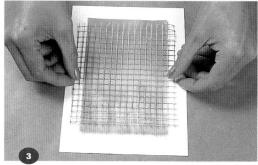

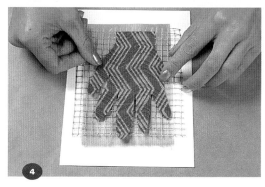

Mixed Media Collage #2

1. Assemble the materials that you plan to combine into a collage, and trim the flat ones with scissors or a mat knife into shapes for layering (photo 1, right). (We used hand-dyed paper, gold mesh screen, folded patterned paper, buttons, and a rock wound with decorative cord.)

2. Arrange the components into a collage that allows portions of each material to show underneath the others (photos 2 through 5). Attach the pieces with an adhesive of your choice (see pages 20 through 24).

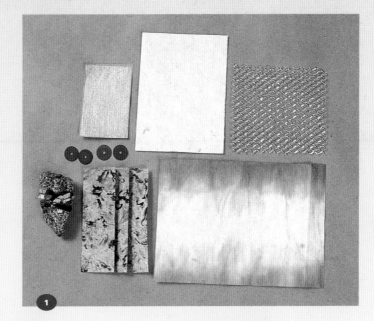

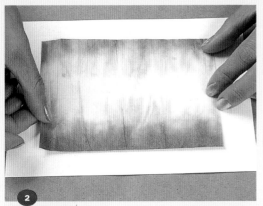

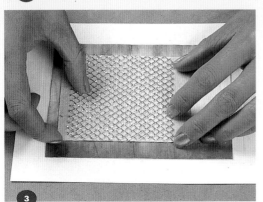

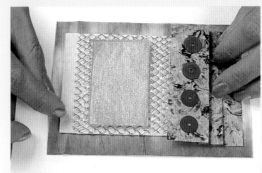

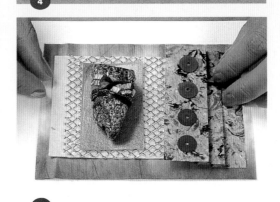

Composing

WORKING INTUITIVELY

Collage is what artists call a "process-oriented" art. Simply expressed, this means that the process involved in creating a collage has as much value as the end result. Artists who are drawn to improvisation, or inventing a large part of the work as they go along, find collage to be a natural outlet—just as some musicians are drawn to jazz.

If you've never taken up drawing or painting because you were intimidated by the thought of trying to render a likeness of

something, you may find that collage will help you shed your inhibitions about trying your hand at an artistic activity.

The process of making a collage doesn't have to be complicated, nor does any of it have to be "perfect." In fact, the word perfect doesn't really come into play in this process. Collage allows you to cancel worries about the outcome, and allow all sorts of fortuitous "accidents" to occur that make the work better. Giving yourself the freedom to create in this way is not a lot different than how you played when you were a child. You didn't worry about making things look a certain way with your tempera paints; you simply enjoyed experimenting with color, texture, and line.

So, before you begin composing your collage, adopt a childlike attitude, and spread your treasures out on your work surface. Allow yourself to take in and enjoy all the colors and textures that you've accumulated. Let your mind wander. Soon you'll begin to make natural, unforced associations between materials that can lead you to ideas for your collage.

After you've established some basic material choices, you may find that the collage begins to develop in your mind. Tear or cut papers, fabrics, or other materials into shapes that can be moved around on the surface. Arrange pieces in many different configurations to discover one that feels right. Stand back from the work, and view it from afar to see patterns that are emerg-

Steve Aimone, *Paper Events 97-3*, 1997, Manipulated paper on poplar board, 11¼ x 11¼ x 1½ in. (28.5 x 28.5 x 3.8 cm)

ing or spots that need attention. Enliven the surface with punctuation points, such as a bright colored material among a group of muted ones, or a swatch of gold leaf among a group of common, commercial papers.

Soon you'll find your own way of working that uses your intuitive, process-oriented side.

WORKING FROM AN IMAGE

If you feel more comfortable with planning than improvising, you may end up enjoying the process of making collages that are derived from a representational image. Many artists use a preexisting image or draw their own before "painting" it with bits of paper, fabric, or other material. Working with a preconceived image gives you guidelines, but still allows you to be spontaneous within that framework.

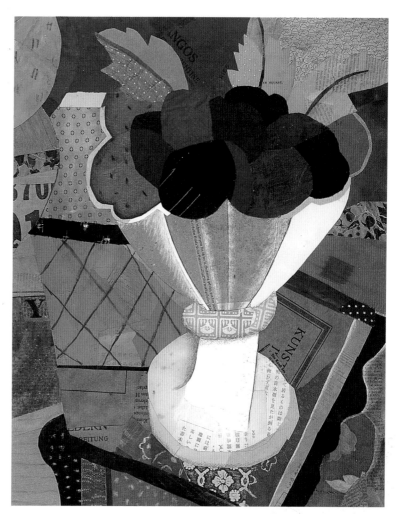

Pia Öste-Alexander, *Plums*, 1994, Collaged papers and fabric with charcoal drawing, 16 x 20 in. (40.6 x 50.8 cm)

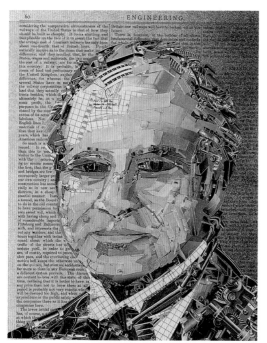

Jonathan Talbot, *John Lehman, Engineer*, 1999, Collage of found papers from 19th century engineering journals on watercolor paper, Image: 9¾ x 8 in. (24.8 x 20.3 cm)

DESIGN BASICS

Have you ever wondered what the heck painters were doing when they paused, stepped back dramatically from their canvases, and squinted? They're working at the design of their composition. By stepping back and looking at the forest instead of the trees, they're able to tweak their designs. They can see how individual elements that they've combined influence one another.

If you think that you don't know anything about design, you may be surprised to find out how much you actually *do* know. Simply put, the subject of design in art and craft concerns the arrangement of elements that compose a work of art or craft, and the relationships between those elements in a fundamental framework. Artists often seek to "unify" elements in a composition. By familiarizing yourself with a few basics of design, you'll be able to influence the overall unity of your design.

The following brief descriptions of design basics, described through simple collages created by Steve Aimone, will give you a place to start as you look at the world of design and apply it to your work.

Repetition of Motif

One of the easiest and most obvious ways in which you can create unity in your composition is by repeating a motif. In the

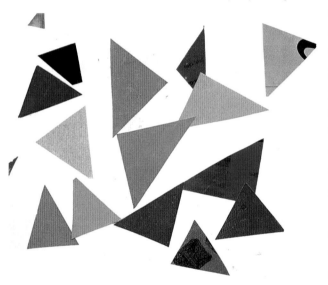

example that you see here, triangles are repeated to make up a composition. Within that framework, the triangles (or compositional elements) are varied in size, color, placement, and orientation. This variety adds visual interest within the united framework created through repeating elements.

Rhythmic Repetition of Motif

This concept is as old as people beating drums around a fire. When you start beating a drum, it's natural to tap it at evenly spaced intervals. After awhile, you may find that boring, so you'll begin to interject variations.

You might tap four even beats, and then add two quick beats. Now you've created a pattern, and you'll probably repeat that pattern for as long as it is interesting to you. Your musical number is unified by the common element of the beat with variations.

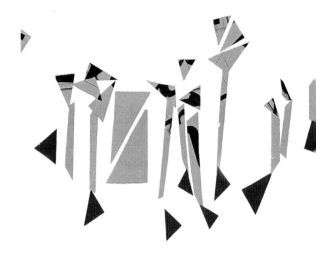

The simple collage that you see here illustrates this idea. It demonstrates unity through the repetition of triangles, and variety through the differences in the shapes and colors of the triangles. Beyond that, the triangles and other shapes are arranged in a sequence of beat-like occurrences. When you look at this composition, it's exciting because it engages your eye in rhythmic movement.

Symmetry

If you ever took a basic art class, you probably learned about symmetry. It's the oldest way of organizing a composition. Look at a Renaissance painting, and you'll almost always find a central axis. Think about your body and how all of the parts of your body radiate out from your spine.

In design, this central axis creates a sense of balance and organization. Visual elements are then placed on either side. In

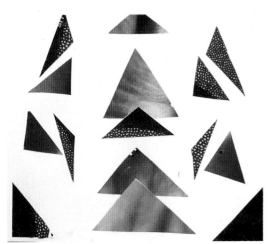

ter of overlapped triangles is placed on one side of the composition. If left as is, this "cloud" might seem ungrounded and unbalanced. So the artist has consciously placed three triangles on the other side of the composition to counterbalance this grouping. Two of these triangles bleed off the edges of the composition, creating a visual force that eventually pulls the eye away from the cluster of triangles and equalizes the two realms of the composition.

the composition that you see here, the central triangles form an axis, and mirror-like components complement this axis. To create visual excitement, these components are not precise mirrors of one another, but close enough to retain the stability that is so characteristic of symmetry.

Asymmetry

Simply put, asymmetry is a way of organizing without a central axis. Many Renaissance artists considered this idea to be the antithesis of visual organization, while ancient Zen artists found delight in this way of thinking. Contemporary artists who create abstract compositions often lean toward asymmetrical arrangements. In the piece that you see here, a large clus-

Focal Point

Many compositions end up having one main point of interest, often called the focal point, that first engages the eye. This "anchor spot" creates a sense of stability and rest in the composition. In the example shown here, your eye is encouraged to roam around the composition from point to point before resting on the patterned red triangle near the center.

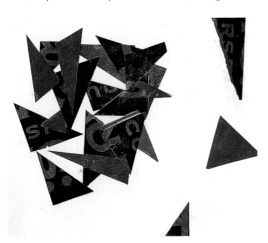

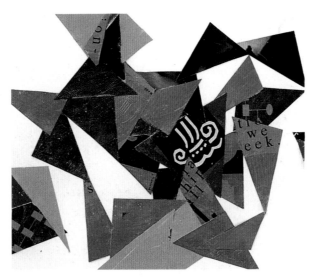

A focal point can be created in many ways—it can be as simple as a black dot in the middle of a field of white ones. When you create a composition of any sort, you'll probably find that you establish a focal point naturally.

Warming Up to Your Work

Playing with shapes in an informal manner is a great way to warm up to your work, get your creative juices flowing, and begin composing.

Artist Steve Aimone uses paper collage as a vehicle for teaching design and composition. He believes that working with cut and pasted shapes frees a person from limited notions about art. (Such as the outmoded belief that you've got to be able to draw, paint, or sculpt in order to participate in the process of art).

In the following exercise, he shows how triangles cut from a variety of papers can be improvisationally developed into a simple collage.

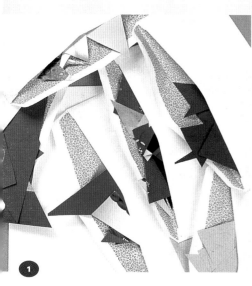

To do this, you'll need a variety of commercial papers in different colors, scissors, a paintbrush, a piece of heavy paper to serve as a support, and acrylic paint in colors of your choice. You can apply the pieces with wet adhesive (acrylic medium or white craft glue) as shown in this demonstration, or use the dry method described by Jonathan Talbot on pages 22 through 24.

1. Cut a series of triangular shapes from newspapers, magazines, or colored papers. (If you're using the dry method of applying the pieces the support, follow the steps outlined for coating the papers with acrylic medium before cutting them into triangles.) Separate the triangles by color into a series of envelopes (photo 1). By limiting yourself to triangular shapes, your composition will have natural unity.

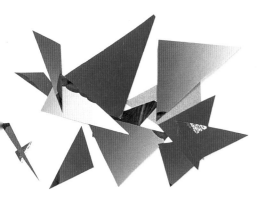

2. Choose one of the envelopes and empty some of the triangles out onto the paper support (photo 2). If you like the way that the pieces fall, begin with this arrangement of elements. If you don't, shuffle the pieces around until you like the arrangement. If you're using wet adhesive, use the paintbrush and acrylic medium or glue to attach the pieces to the paper (photo 3).

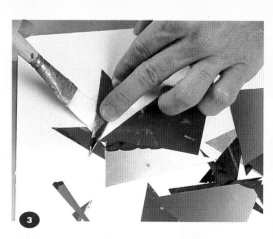

3. Add pieces to the composition that are of a complementary color (photo 4). Here, we've added yellow pieces to the purple pieces. (Other complementary combinations include red/green and orange/blue.) When you place these colors side by side,

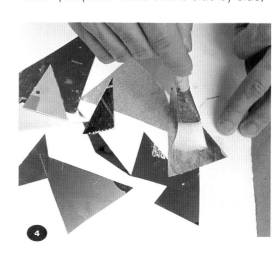

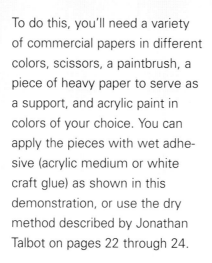

they activate one another through sharp contrast.

4. Add more triangular components to the composition to produce variety and tension. Here, we've added fragments of hard-edged text, bits of black, and touches of red to create additional points of interest in the composition (photo 5). Add pieces until you find a satisfying composition—one that feels balanced, unified, and rhythmic. Keep in mind that there are an infinite number of ways to arrange the elements and make a successful composition.

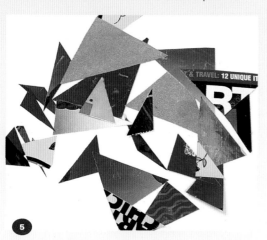

5. If you've applied a wet adhesive, you can add visual interest to the composition by ripping several of the triangles off of the support to leave fragile paper remnants (photo 6). You've now employed

the element of chance into your composition, since you don't know exactly what will be left when you pull the paper from the support.

6. If you feel that you've created too much clutter, you can paint in areas over the composition. Here, a passage of the design is masked off with white paint to create empty space. Notice how this "calms down" the composition (photo 7). The paper underneath the paint adds texture and richness to the composition.

7. If you want, add more paint to mask other areas of the design. Try using a paint color that complements your design (we've used purple). Add a small cutout shape on top of one of the painted areas for contrast (photo 8). Here, we've added a contrasting yellow triangle on top of the purple paint. Continue with this process of layering, stripping away, and painting until you're satisfyed with your improvisational composition (photo 9).

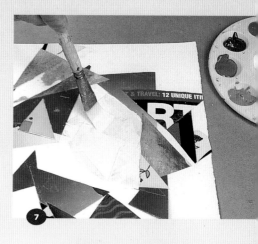

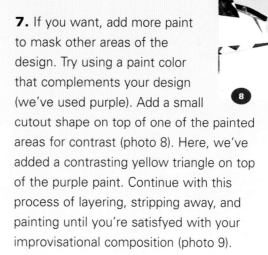

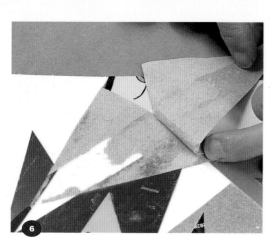

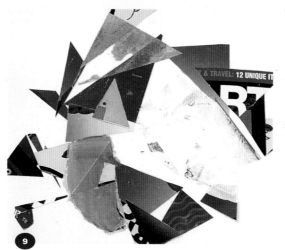

Embellishing the Surface

YOU CAN ADD COLOR TO PAPER (and some fabrics) with any coloring medium that you choose—paint, dyes, crayons, colored pencils, chalks. Add color before cutting or tearing paper or fabric, or add color after you've assembled the collage.

If you plan to use paints, they have different characteristics. Oil paints are heavy and opaque when they come out of the tube. They can be used in this form or

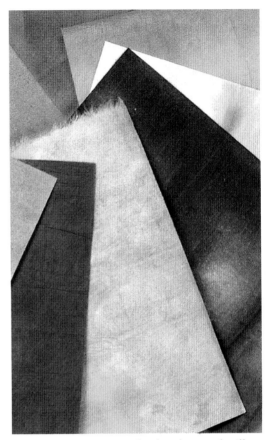

Some papers are extremely absorbent and will soak up paint or dye easily.

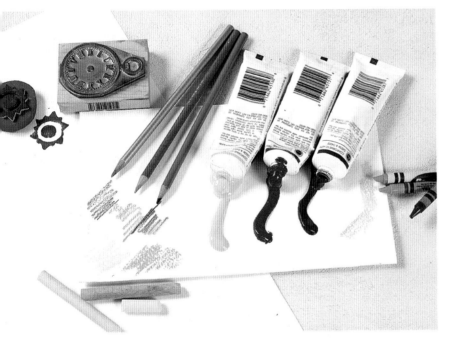

Add color to paper with stamps, colored pencils, paints, chalks, or crayons.

thinned with turpentine to make washes. If you choose traditional oil paint, remember that it takes hours to dry. Acrylic paint out of the tube dries quickly to create an opaque, matte surface. It can also be thinned with water and used as a wash or stain for the surface of your collage. Watercolor paints are perfect for adding delicate tinges of color to absorbent papers.

When adding color to paper with paint, keep in mind that papers vary greatly in their absorbency. Some papers, such as Japanese papers or watercolor papers, are extremely absorbent and will soak up your paint easily. Coated papers, such as photocopies and magazine cutouts, won't absorb paint as readily. Try a sample of your paper and paint together before you apply it to a composition that you've worked on for some time.

To further alter the surface, paint an area of your collaged surface with oil or acrylic paint, and use the end of your paintbrush

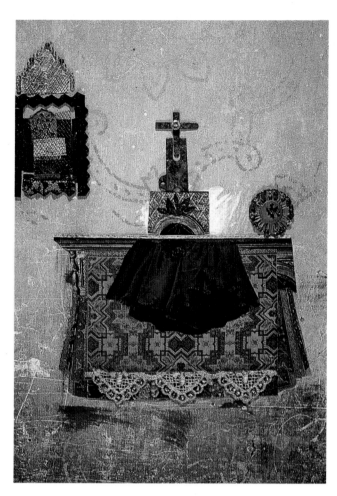

maker's brayer or roller on a small sheet of glass or other hard surface (you can roll out the paint on glossy magazine pages in a pinch). Roll an even coat of paint onto the stamp, and print it on top of your collaged surface to add more dimension and texture. You can also ink the stamp from a rubber stamp pad, but it won't supply the rich surface that paint does.

As you begin to think about stamping designs, you'll realize that you can put paint on any surface that will hold it and use it to press designs onto the surface. Leaves, keys, window screen, or anything that will clean up afterwards or can be thrown away will work. This technique offers a lot of room for experimentation and surprise. Simple stencils of lettering or other designs can be purchased at craft supply stores, and used to add components to your collage. Make your own stencils by cutting shapes out of heavy paper with a mat knife fitted with a thicker blade.

to make marks on the surface before the paint has dried. You can also stamp or stencil the surface of your collage with paint. To apply the paint to a stamp (rubber or otherwise), roll it out with a print-

Left: Brigid Burns, *Introibo Ad Altare Deum*, 1994, Mixed media collage with oil, newsprint, gold stamp, fabric, metal, rubber, and glass beads applied to photograph, 8 x 10 in. (20.3 x 25.4 cm)

Below: Sharon McCartney, *The Quiet Ones Are Easily Overlooked*, 1999, Mixed media with watercolor, collage, and encaustic,13 x 40 in. (33 x 101.6 cm)

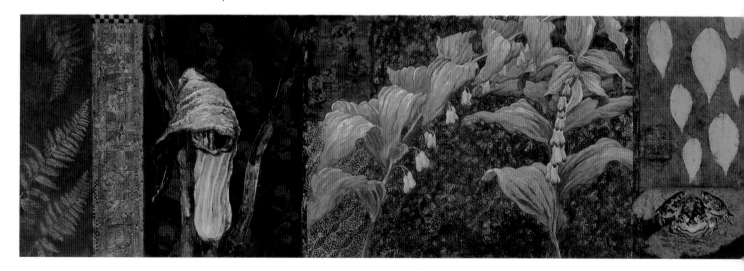

Gallery

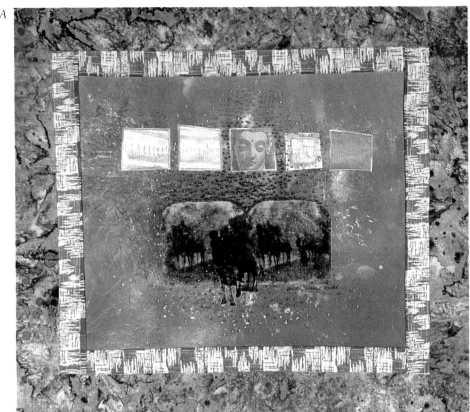

A   Sandra T. Donabed, *Migration*,
1999, Fabric collage made with canvas printed with oil paint from lucite
plate and photo gel transfer,
24 x 21 in. (61 x 53.3 cm)

B   Roscoe C. Conn, Jr., *Pool Room*,
1999, Collage and mixed media,
14 x 18 in. (35.6 x 45.7 cm),
Courtesy of Blue Spiral Gallery:
Asheville, North Carolina

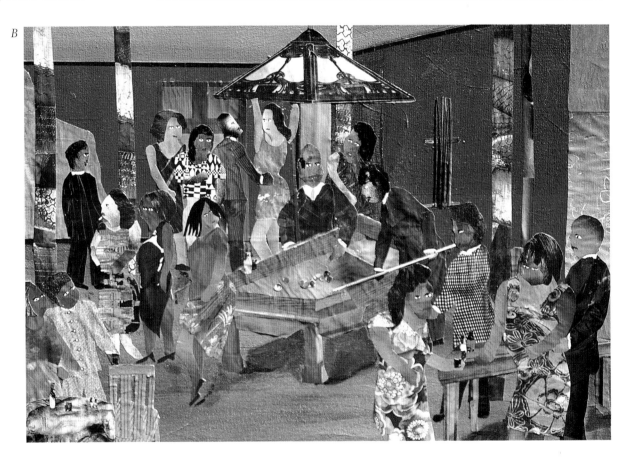

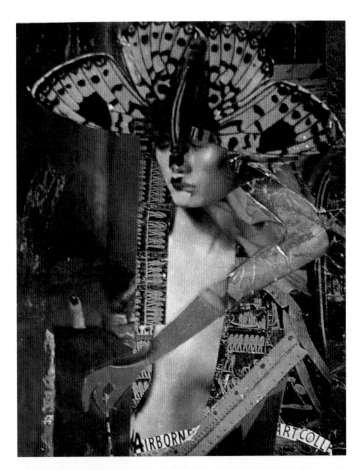

C Gennielynn Martin, *Full of Certainty*,
  c. 1999, Collage with color photocopies,
  gold leaf, varnish/crackle medium,
  14 x 16 in. (35.6 x 40.6 cm)

D Niki Bonnett, *American in Asia*, 1996,
  Collage with fabric, paper photocopies,
  acetate photocopies, luggage tags,
  brochure photos, found objects,
  53 x 83 in. (124.6 x 210 cm)

D

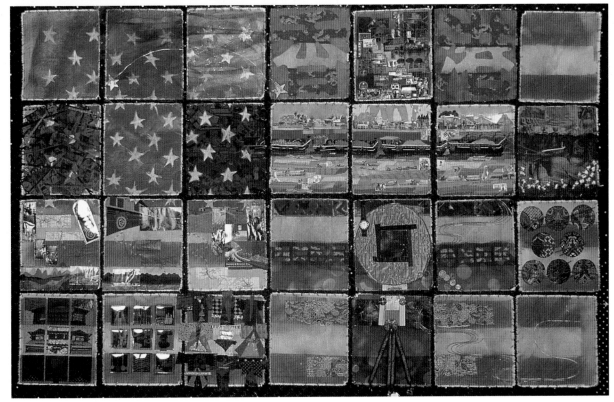

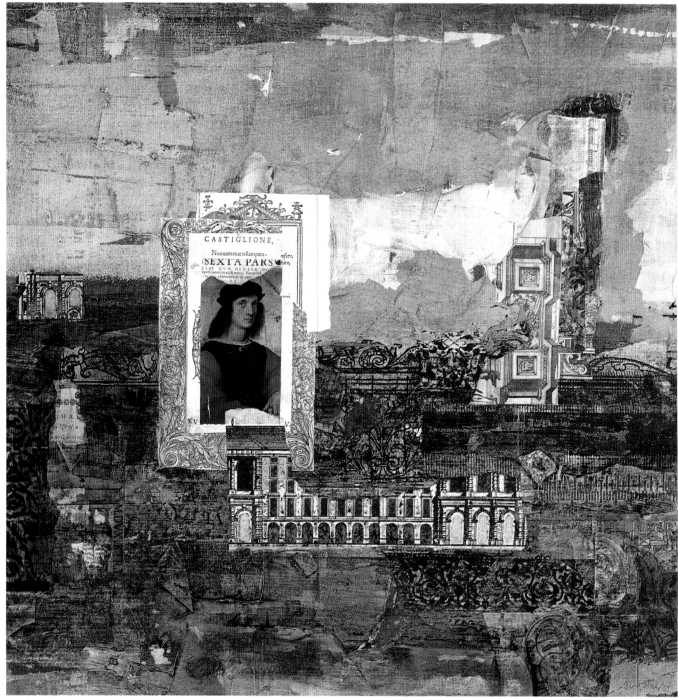

Fred Otnes, *Castiglione*, Mixed media collage, 2000, 23 x 23 in. (58.4 x 58.4 cm)

A Carole Bleistein, *Asian Daily News*, 1996,
   Collage with Japanese papers, Japanese
   newsprint, coconut strands, tree bark, tissue paper, handpainted paper,
   12 x 15 in. (30.5 x 38.1 cm)

B Ann Hartley, *Flat Land*, 1987, Mixed-
   media collage, 22 x 30 in. (55.9 x 76.2 cm)

C Claudine Hellmuth, *The Fish in the Zodiac*,
   1998, Mixed media collage with acrylic,
   watercolor, and antique papers, 6 x 9 in.
   (15.2 x 22.9 cm)

A
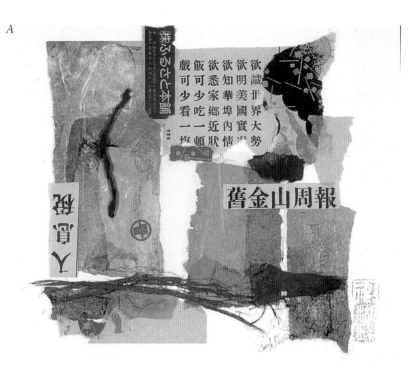

B
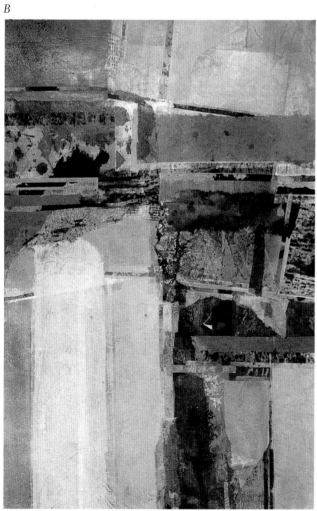

C
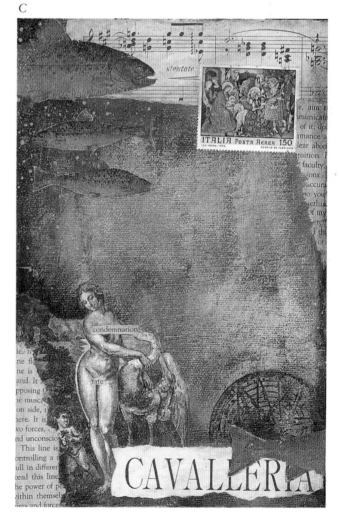

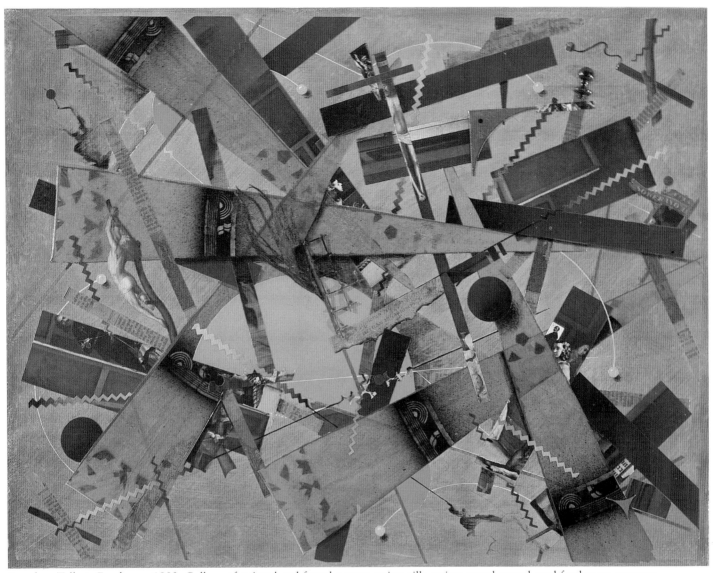

Jonathan Talbot, *Fandango*, 1992, Collage of painted and found papers, paint, silk, string, metal, wood, and feather on museum board mounted on watercolor paper, Image: 15½ x 20 in. (39.4 x 50.8 cm), Paper: 22 x 26 in. (55.9 x 66 cm)

A Ann Hartley, *Homecoming*, 1995, Collage with acrylic, paper, stitchery, and metal, 12 x 12 in. (30.5 x 30.5 cm)

B Heather Allen, *36 Ponder Art Quilt*, 1998, Cotton, linen, silk, dye, and textile ink. 66 x 29 in. (167.6 x 73.7 cm)

C Darcy Falk, *Refuge*, 1999, Commercial and hand-dyed cotton and silk fabrics, thread, and batting. Layered, 27 x 21½ in. (68.6 x 54.6 cm)

A

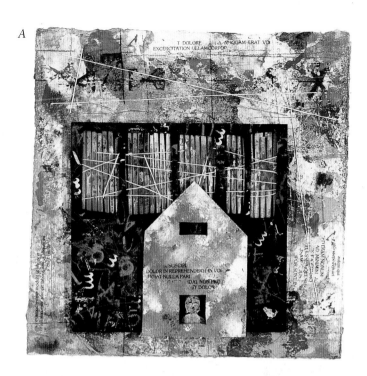

B

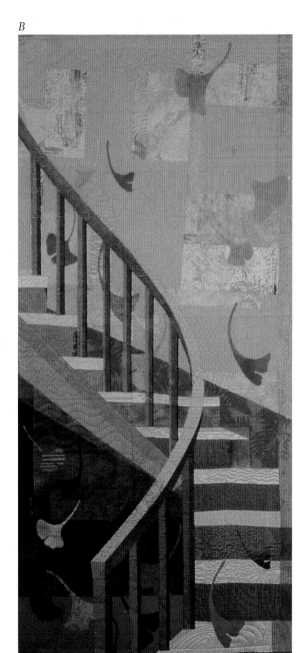

C

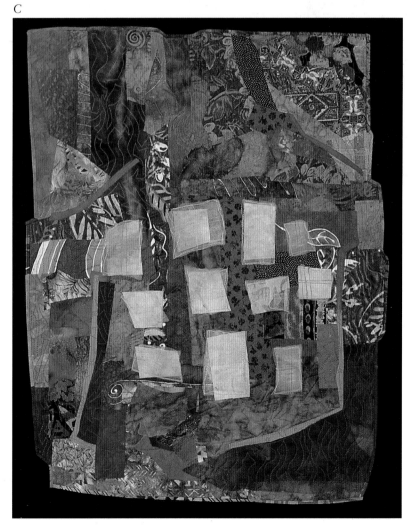

A

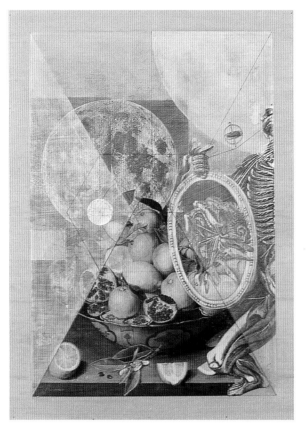

B

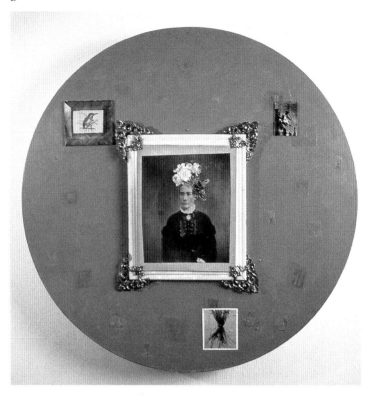

A Michael Mew, *Still Life*, 1996, Mixed media collage on paper mounted on board, 33 x 24 in. (83.8 x 61 cm)

B Lisa Tuttle, *Anna's Daybook*, 1999, Paper collage, acrylic, wooden and metal frame, photograph, wax, beveled glass, on glass over wood, 28 in. (71.1 cm) diameter

C Aleta Braun/Robert Ebendorf, *Life Cycle*, 1998, Mixed media collage, 3¾ x 3¾ x 1¼ in. (9.5 x 9.5 x 3.2 cm)

C

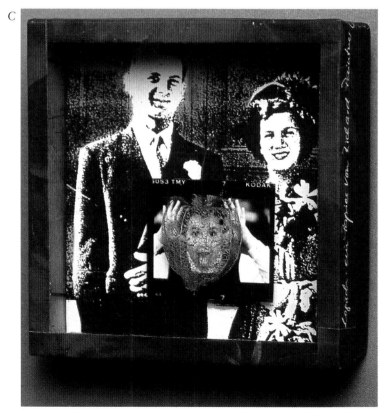

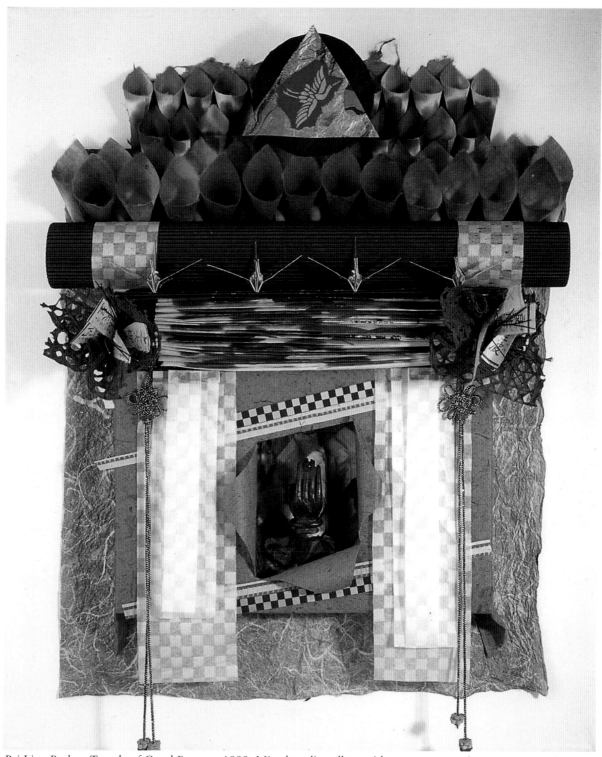

Pei Ling Becker, *Temple of Good Fortune*, 1999, Mixed media collage with paper constructions, knotted silk chord, carved jade, and beads, 24 x 28 in. (61 x 71.1 cm)

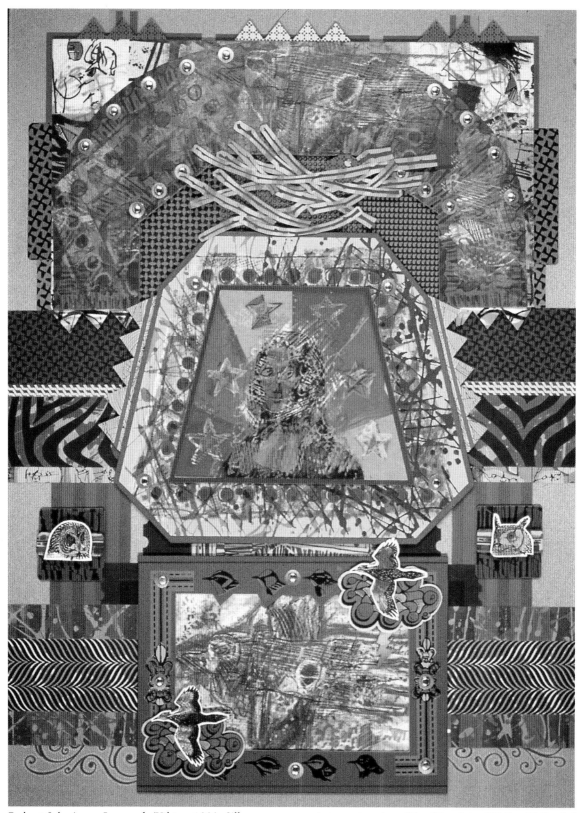

Robert Schwieger, *Leonardo/Viktor*, 1999, Silkscreen monoprint construction, 27 x 20 x 1 in. (68.6 x 50.8 x 2.5 cm)

Projects

THE FOLLOWING SECTION CONTAINS ideas for using collage in unexpected ways. These inspirational projects contain sections listing the materials and tools as well as the process for each. Keep in mind that you won't be recreating any of these ideas precisely, but the instructions will provide you with enough information to make a similar piece of your own.

The nature of collage is open-ended. Use your own personal materials and ideas to delve into the creative process and allow your imagination to lead you by the hand.

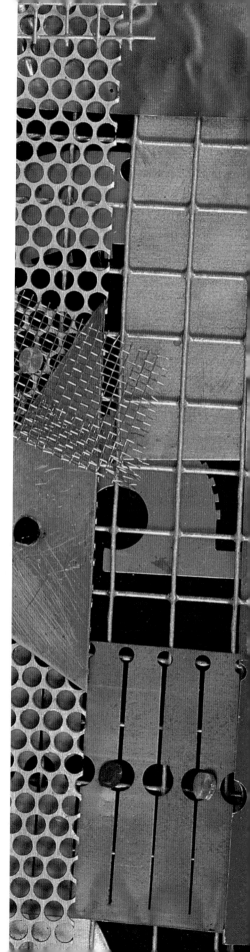

Just for Fun Cards

MATERIALS AND TOOLS

Blank cards and envelopes

Old travel postcards from thrift shops and yard sales

Small, unusual objects, such as small plastic toys, metal charms, stones, flea market costume jewelry

Decorative paper punch

Postage stamps

Metallic embroidery floss

Colored papers

Acrylic paint

Sponge

White craft glue

Scissors

Designer
Barbara Evans

MAKE FANCIFUL COLLAGED CARDS from old postcards and trinkets to send to a friend. They're easy to make, and a joy to receive.

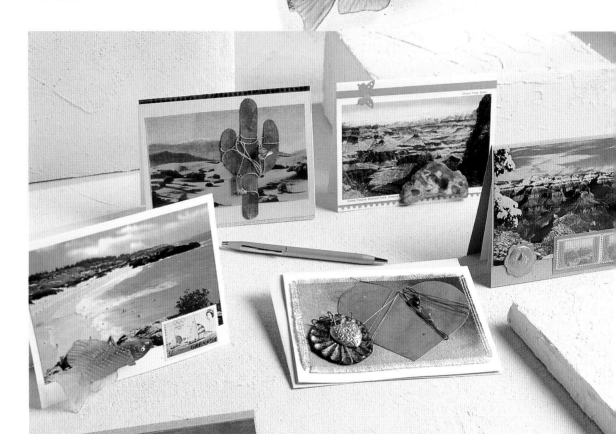

PROCESS

Create small collages on blank cards from old postcards combined with decorative and colored papers, small objects, and postage stamps. Sponge papers with acrylic paint to create interesting effects. Add shapes punched with a decorative paper punch of your choice or metallic embroidery thread to enhance your design.

Traveler's Trove

AN OLD THIFTSHOP SUITCASE CAN become a canvas for sentimental ticket stubs, receipts, and other mementos from journeys.

PROCESS

Tear out large pages from magazines or newspapers that have images that you like. Coat the backs of the pages with acrylic medium, and press them into place on the surface of the suitcase. Use these sheets as the background for your design. Add sheets of patterned paper to this first layer. Press out air bubbles as you go. Allow this portion of the collage to dry.

Arrange paper memorabilia on top of this background until you create a composition that you like. Brush the backs of the pieces with acrylic medium, and press them into place. (Notice that the designer has used only a few components to make an effective composition.)

After the next layer of paper has dried, apply two to three coats of acrylic medium to the surface of the collage as a sealer. Allow it to dry to a hard finish. **Note:** You can opt to use the dry adhesive method described on pages 22 through 24 to apply the collage components.

MATERIALS AND TOOLS

Old thriftshop suitcase

Magazine or newspaper pages

Patterned paper

Travel memorabilia such as hotel receipts, receipts for museum and opera tickets, luggage tags, airline tickets

Acrylic matte medium

Paintbrush

Designer
Ellen Zahorec

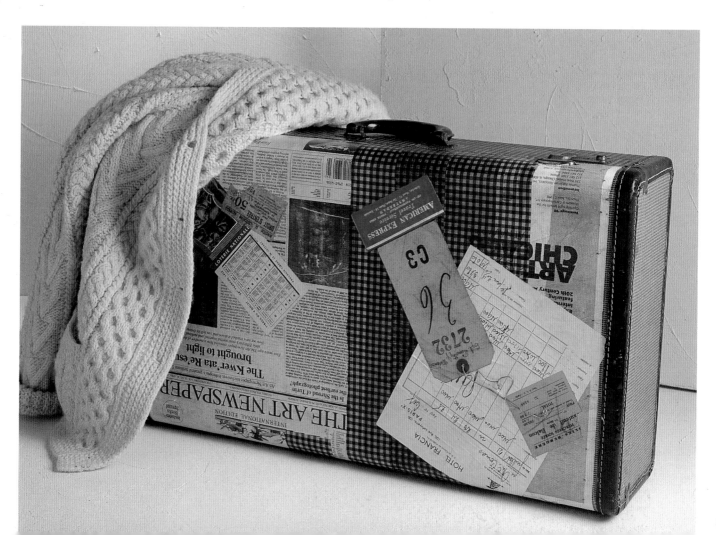

Checkerboard

MATERIALS AND TOOLS

Piece of 16-inch-square (40 x 40 cm) heavy board (such as illustration board, plywood, or foam core)

Pencil

Ruler

Low-tack masking tape

Acrylic paint in two colors that complement the images you choose for your board (see instructions)

Scrap paper

Small sea sponge (or other sponge for decorative painting)

Dictionary

32 images from thrift shop books or magazines (such as gems, flowers, or animals) not exceeding 1¾ inches (4.4 cm) each

Scissors

Sheet of heavy paper

Rubber cement

Spray fixative

Wax paper

Stack of books

¼-inch (6 mm) sheet of clear plastic sheeting that measures 1½ x 48 inches (3.8 x 121 cm) cut into 32 squares (don't remove the protective plastic), or set of 32 storebought checkers

Small paintbrush

Designer
Terry Taylor

THIS CLEVER CHECKERBOARD WAS created using vintage gem and mineral illustrations from a volume of an old encyclopedia found at a thrift shop. Definitions of each gem or mineral were photocopied from a dictionary to accompany the illustrations. Create your own gameboard with any theme that you like—the possibilities are limitless.

PROCESS

Use a pencil and a ruler to draw a line 1 inch (2.5 cm) inside the perimeter of the square of heavy board to create a border. Within this border, mark off a grid that defines 64 squares that each measure 1¾ x 1¾ inches (4.4 x 4.4 cm).

Use masking tape to mask the inside of the border on all sides. Squeeze out a small amount of one of the two colors of acrylic paint on a piece of scrap paper, and gently dab the sponge in the paint.

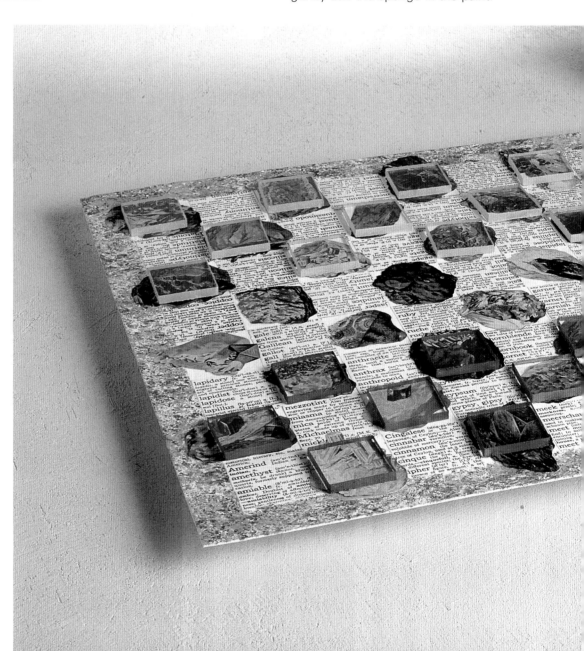

Sponge the border to create a mottled effect. Allow the paint to dry, then sponge the second color on top of the first.

Use a photocopy machine to make copies of words and definitions related to your board theme from a dictionary. Enlarge the definitions so that they cover the squares and can be read easily (don't worry if they extend beyond the size slightly). You'll need 32 definitions for 32 squares. Allow words that appear before and after your chosen definitions to show as a part of the design.

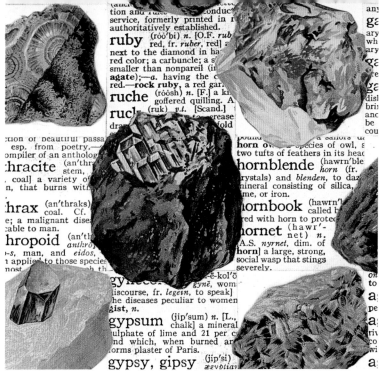

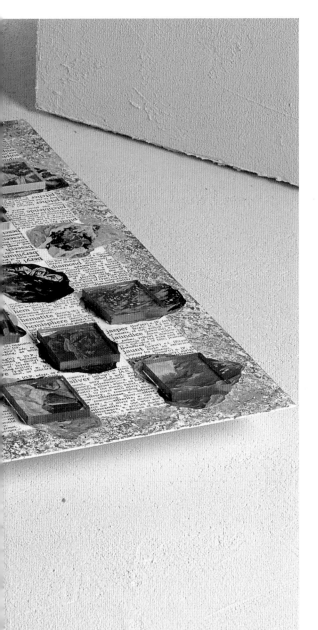

Use scissors to cut out the 32 images from books and magazines. Cut around the natural shapes of the images, or cut them into squares that fit onto the board. Cut a 1¾ inch (4.4 cm) square template from the sheet of heavy paper. Use this template to trace the borders of both the images and the definitions so that they'll fit on the squares.

Lay your images and definitions on sheets of newspaper, and spray one side followed by the other with spray fixative to prevent smearing or image bleed-through. Brush rubber cement on the backs of the images and the definitions. Glue them to the board, matching up the definitions with the images. Cover the board with sheets of wax paper, place several heavy books on top, and allow the board to dry overnight.

If you're using clear plastic squares for your gameboard instead of store-bought checkers, paint the edges of 16 of them with one color of acrylic paint, and paint the edges of the other 16 with the other color. Peel off the protective paper after you've painted the edges.

Patterned Lamp Shade

MATERIALS AND TOOLS

Old dress pattern

Paper lamp shade

Acrylic matte medium

Paintbrush

Designer
Ellen Zahorec

LIGHT UP AN OLD LAMPSHADE WITH the most unexpected of materials: the printed sheets of a dress pattern.

PROCESS

Cut the tissue paper sheets of an old dress pattern into segments. Paint a coat of acrylic medium over a portion of the surface of the lamp shade. Begin pressing the pattern segments onto the shade, and smooth them into place with more medium and a brush.

Continue to add pieces over the surface of the shade, layering them as you go to create interesting designs. After you are satisfied with the surface, coat the shade with a final coat of acrylic medium to seal it.

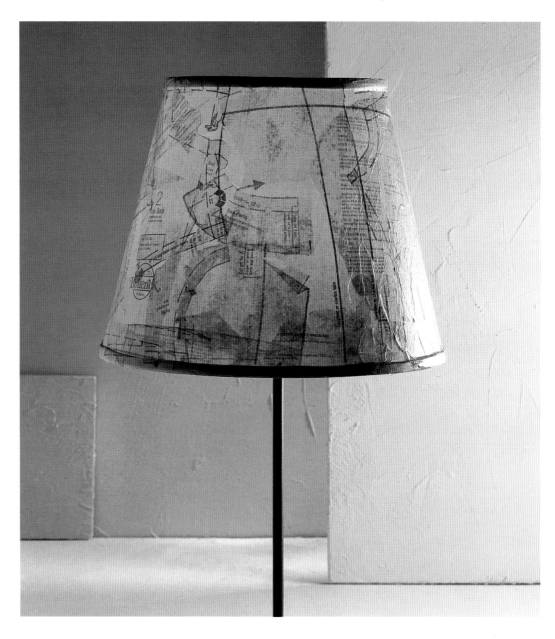

Musical Notes

CREATE A SERIES of collaged note cards by beginning with an old piece of sheet music.

PROCESS

Paint the sheet music with a coat of crackle varnish followed by a coat of gold paint. After the paper dries, tear it into small, randomly-sized pieces.

Tear the handmade and textured papers into pieces. To prepare the leaves, dilute a small amount of white craft glue with water. Paint the front and back of each leaf with the glue, and allow it to dry.

Layer papers, netting, and leaves onto the front of each card to form a small, simple collage. Glue them into place. Add gold and silver paint to the background of some of the cards.

MATERIALS AND TOOLS

Blank note cards and matching envelopes

Old sheet music or other printed paper with a theme

Crackle-finish varnish

Gold and silver paint for paper

Paintbrushes

Handmade or textured papers

Fresh leaves

White craft glue

Netting or other widely woven fabric

Pieces of paper doilies

*Designer
Nancy Worrell*

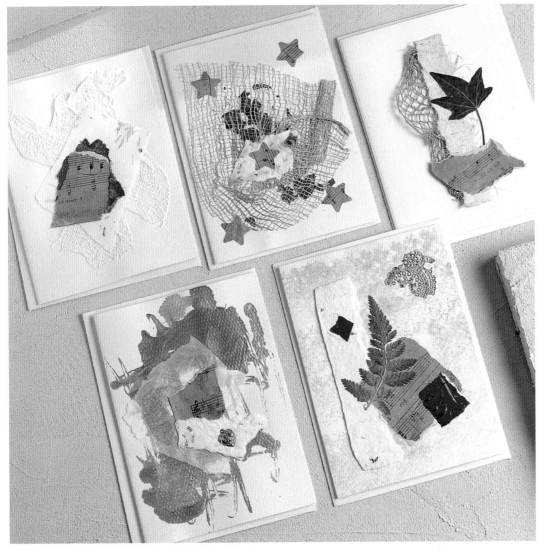

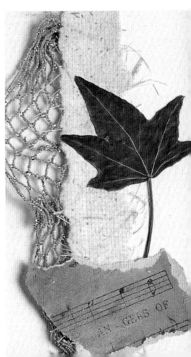

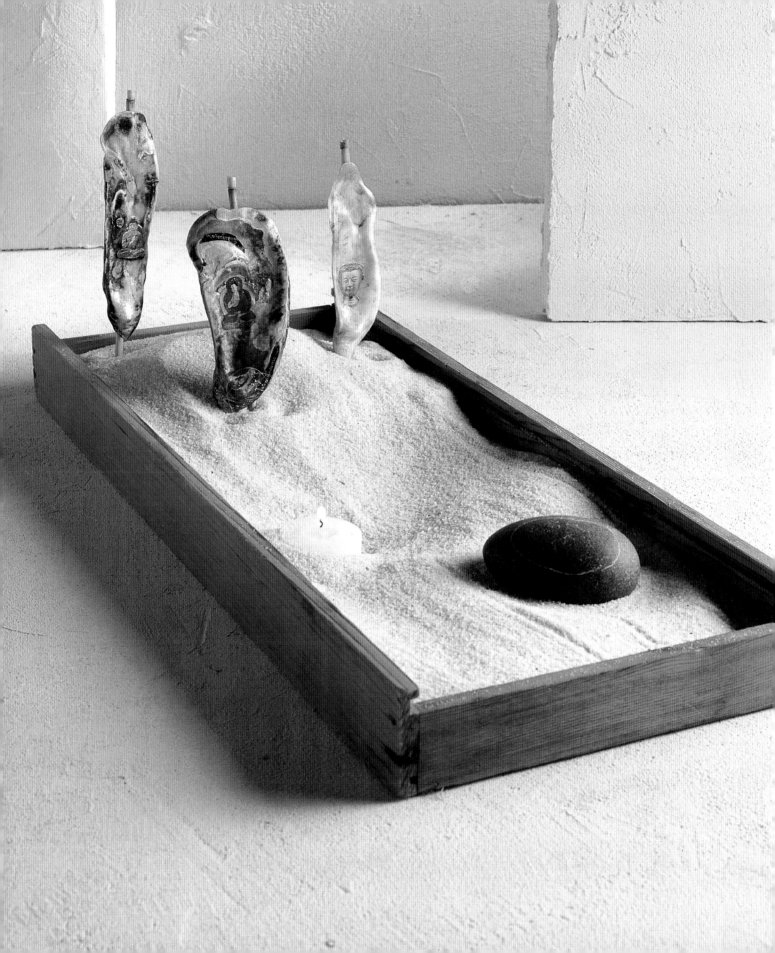

Oyster Altar

THE ARTIST BEGAN THIS PIECE WITH THE SEED OF AN IDEA. She wondered if she might be able to integrate images into the curved interiors of shells without compromising the natural beauty of the forms. Her first attempts at this process produced subtle results that weren't very interesting, so she added more colorful images that were meaningful to her.

The results of her experimentation transformed her collaged surfaces into miniature icons. After completing the shells, she wanted a way in which to display them and arrived at the solution of a sand-filled altar in which the pieces could be arranged and rearranged.

PROCESS

Clean debris or sand from the shells and dry them thoroughly. Cut small images from magazines and other print media with the small scissors and/or a mat knife.

Arrange the images in the curves of the shells, and glue them into place with decoupage glue. Smooth the paper with your fingers. Add small bits of tissue paper or other thin papers to the collages. Choose images with shapes and colors that integrate well with the curved surfaces of the shells. Add bits of color around the images with colored markers, paints, or chalk pastels. Further enhance the pieces with materials such as rub-on gold leaf and tissue paper.

When you're satisfied with the work you've done on each shell, allow the glue to dry thoroughly. Paint a coat of acrylic medium on top of each of the collages to seal it and give it a sheen.

Cut off pieces of reed or a thin dowel that are long enough to attach to the back of each of the shells with an excess of 2 to 3 inches (5 to 7.5 cm) at the bottom. Squeeze out a line of thick, tacky glue onto the back of each shell, and lay the reed or dowel on the glue. Allow the glue to set.

Fill the box with sand, and spread it around with your hands or a medium-sized paintbrush to create gentle hills and valleys. Prop the shells up in the sand at one end, then add the candle and the rock to create a small altar.

MATERIALS AND TOOLS

Oyster shells and other shells

Assorted found papers from magazines, newspapers, and other sources

Rub-on gold leaf

Tissue paper or other thin, semi-transparent paper

Small scissors

Mat knife

Decoupage glue

Acrylic gloss medium

Colored markers, paint, or chalk pastels

Small paintbrush

Pieces of thin reed or thin dowel

Thick, tacky glue

Shallow wooden box

Sand

Votive candle

Smooth rounded river rock

Designer
Carolyn Brooks

Blind Jean Box

THE ARTIST SAYS THAT THIS COLLAGE/ASSEMBLAGE created itself in a stream-of-consciousness manner. Layers of old cotton batting gently protect the treasures in her box.

MATERIALS AND TOOLS

Old wooden box

Old cotton batting, velvet, or other soft material

Shells, jewelry, or other objects

Old papers such as sheet music and letters

Craft knife or scissors

Acrylic matte medium

Paintbrush

Fountain pen filled with india ink

Designer
Rose Kelly

PROCESS

To create your own piece by a process of free association, first make an environment for words, papers, and objects inside a box. Layer the bottom of the box with old cotton or other soft material, and place within it objects that hold special significance for you.

Use the lid to create a collage of words, remnants of personal letters, photos, or costume jewelry. Apply the pieces of the collage with acrylic matte medium. Add words to the objects or to the collage by writing them with a pen filled with india ink.

It never ceases to amaze me when disparate items in my studio seem to gravitate to one another during the process of creating an art piece such as this one.

One day at a library, I jotted down a phrase from a book on a card from a defunct card catalogue. On the other end of the card was written the name "Blind, Jean." Later, an old box that I found conjured up the phrase, "toujours, sans exception, sans doute, pour l'eternite" (always, without exception, without doubt, for eternity). In my mind, I connected these words to the phrase "blind Jean."

Several luminous shells in my possession provided sequestered spaces on which to write the words of the poem. It seems to me that the words lie inside the shells waiting to be discovered like pearls, while fate also waits for the imaginary 'Jean' to lose her blindness to love.

—Rose Kelly

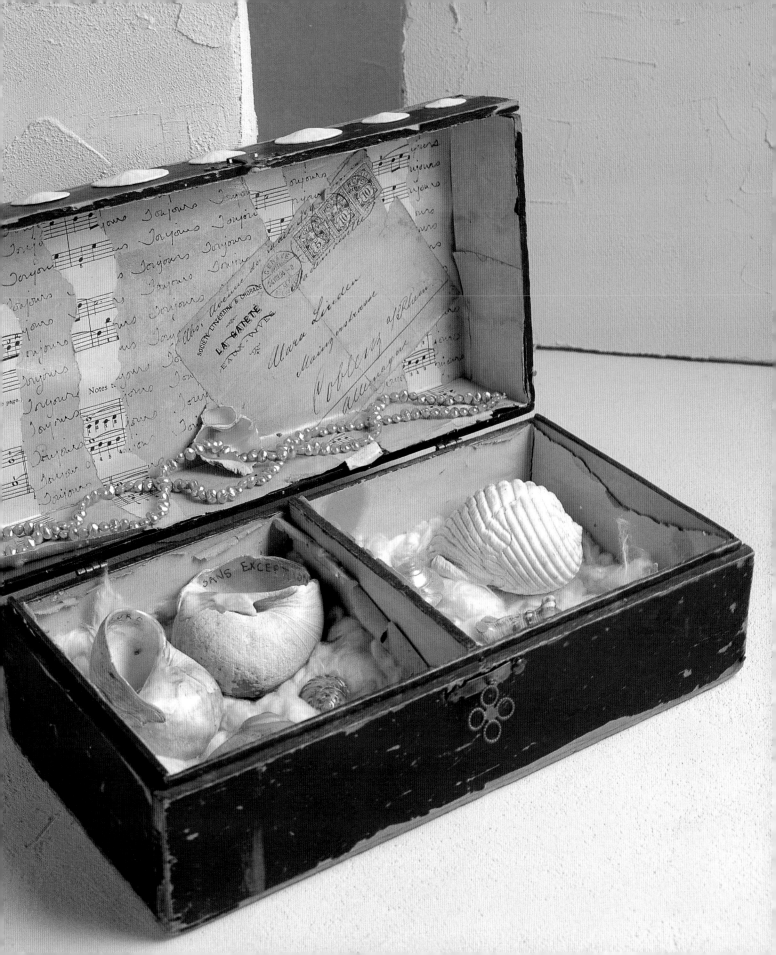

Mail Art Collage

MATERIALS AND TOOLS

Mat knife

Metal ruler

Mat board in color of your choice

Foamboard

Pencil

Dark colored masking tape or cloth tape

Dark colored marker

Sheet of clear plastic (a report cover from an office supply store will work)

Masking tape

Collage components such as photos, letters, maps, magazine pictures, newspaper clippings, and small objects

Double-sided tape

White craft glue

Materials for decorating the outside of the piece: scraps of colored paper or decorative papers cut with regular and decorative-edged scissors, rubber stamps and inkpads, small sponges and paint, cancelled postage stamps

Designer
Luan Udell

SEND A COLLAGE THROUGH THE MAIL that won't be ignored! This "giant postcard sandwich," as the designer calls it, is assembled in such a way that it will (probably) survive the mail system unscathed.

Follow the guidelines outlined below, make sure your piece carries the necessary amount of postage, and you shouldn't have any trouble mailing it.

PROCESS

The basic structure of this piece of mail art made from two slices of mat board and the foamboard. Shallow insets for objects and collage are created by cutting windows in the foamboard which are then covered with clear plastic for protection.

To begin, use the metal ruler and a mat knife to cut out a shape from the mat board (such as a rectangle, square, triangle, or trapezoid). If you're unsure of where to begin with size and shape, make a piece that is half the size of a sheet of typing paper. Your shape needs to be large enough to meet postal regulations, but small enough that it doesn't break your budget to mail it. Check with your post office for size restrictions. If your mail art piece is larger than a card, it is considered to be a "flat" by the post office.

Cut out a second identical sheet of mat board if you're cutting out a rectangle, square, or other regular-shaped form. If you're cutting out an odd shape, reverse the template to cut out the second shape,

To make a collage mail art piece, I often start with a poem or song that—in most cases—I've written. (You can use any idea, theme, poem, song or phrase that inspires you.) I usually print it out on a computer on white, colored, or decorative paper. To make white paper look aged, take a small scrap of sponge and ink it with an inkpad before gently sponging the paper. You can also use a photocopy of a special letter, postcard, or a poem from an book.

As the song I've written runs through my head, I think the story behind it, and envision the people and circumstances that it springs from. Then I collect any artifacts, rubberstamp images, postage stamps, or other components that relate thematically to that song. I do a trial layout to determine where each will be placed, and then go to work.

There are many different ways the pieces of a mail art collage can be assembled. My process is extremely intuitive: I simply arrange and rearrange elements until they 'click' into place and seem satisfying to me.

Any mistakes are either covered up or incorporated into the piece. For 'Burial Song,' I collected quite a few objects at the beginning to illustrate my poem about loss. Finally, I chose to use bones, shells, and a sewing awl (artifacts which I make myself out of polymer clay). I decided to display these artifacts as they would be seen in a museum, in order to make the restrained grieving for a beloved woman more poignant. I wanted to show a human story behind this silent display of ancient artifacts.

—Luan Udell

since you'll need to place the wrong sides of the mat board together to keep the colored sides of the board facing out when you assemble the piece.

Next, cut out a piece of foamboard of the same shape but about ⅛ inch (3 mm) larger than the mat board pieces.

Think about what you plan to place in the windows (papers, artifacts, small objects, etc.). Decide on the size and placement of the windows in the finished piece, and sketch them onto the front of one of the

pieces of mat board. Use the metal ruler and mat knife to cut out the windows. (The remaining piece of mat board will serve as the back wall of your piece.)

Place the cut mat board on top of the foamboard section, aligning the edges. Trace the windows with a pencil. Cut them from the foamboard, enlarging them slightly so that they won't show in the final piece. Then line the edges of the windows with the colored tape, so that you can't see the white edges. Darken the white, inside edges of the mat board piece with the

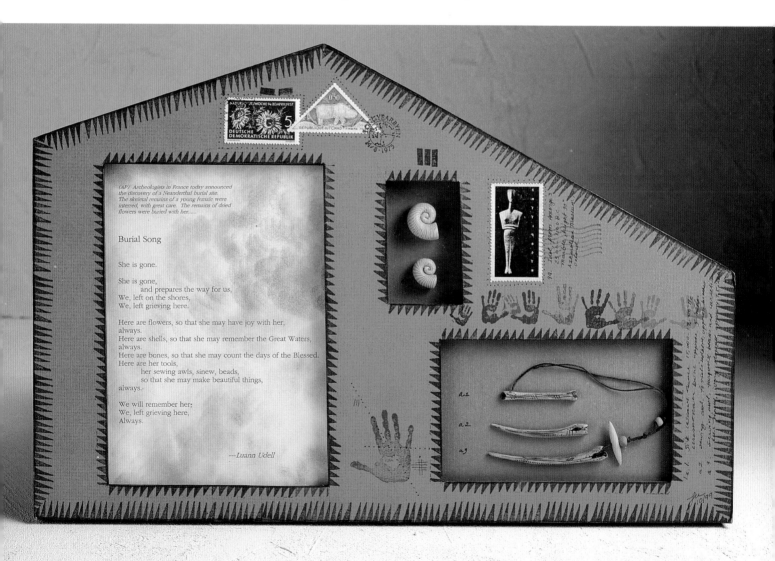

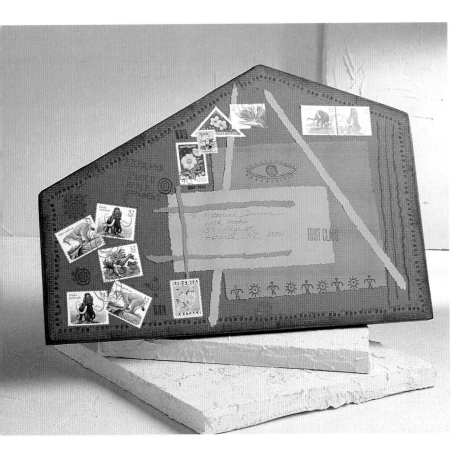

When you've completed your collages inside the windows, place double-sided tape strips about ⅛ inch (3 mm) inside every edge (both outside and cut window edges) on both sides of the foamboard. Line up the edges carefully, and sandwich the three pieces together.

To decorate the front of the piece, rubber stamp the edges with border designs, add handwritten phrases, glue on cancelled postage stamps, or affix other paper components.

Decorate the back side of the piece, but leave plenty of space for an address and postage. If you own a small postage scale, weigh the piece to determine how much postage you'll need so that you can plan the kinds of stamps you'll use (otherwise, you can do this at the post office).

marker. To protect each window, cut a piece of clear plastic about half an inch larger than the openings, and tape it to the underside of the mat with masking tape.

Place the foamboard on the inside of the uncut piece of mat board (the back), and assemble collages inside of each window. If you're using a poem or other written piece, allow the edges of the paper to extend beyond the cutout hole so that they're hidden. Use craft glue to affix artifacts in the windows. While the glue is drying, cover the outside edges of the foamboard with tape, and use the marker to color the outside edges of both mat board pieces.

Incorporate "live" stamps of your choice into the design (ask your postal person to show you a variety of stamps).

Use foreign stamps that are live or cancelled as decoration on the piece (of course, they won't count as real postage). You can also buy these from stamp dealers. Ask dealers to see small packets of what are known as "topicals"—stamps that have similar themes such as flowers, insects, or fairy tales.

To address the work, use rubber stamps, letters cut out from newspapers and glued down, or simply write the name and address of the lucky recipient. Be sure to write in your return address.

Collage Paper Dolls

THESE WHIMSICAL PAPER DOLLS ARE made from a collection of papers that range from magazine clippings to old picture postcards.

PROCESS

Cut out a paper template, using the outline of the doll to the right as a guide. Use a pencil to trace the template several times onto the sheets of heavy paper, and cut out the doll shapes.

Trace portions of each doll onto papers of your choice. (For instance, you might trace the head of the doll onto a portion of an old map, the skirt of the doll onto an old postcard, or create sleeves from a magazine cutout.) Brush the backs of these pieces with glue, and layer them onto the dolls to begin building small collages. Add dresses cut from gift wrap and hats made from maps or postcards. Improvise to come up with your own shapes to serve as hats, vests, or shoes. Use precut paper shapes to further embellish the surface of the dolls.

Note: You can opt to use the dry adhesive method described on pages 22 through 24 to apply the collage components.

MATERIALS AND TOOLS

Pencil

Paper template

Sheets of heavy paper

Scissors

Collection of papers such as old maps, picture postcards, magazine clippings, and gift wraps

Precut decorative paper shapes such as leaves and butterflies from craft store

White craft glue

Paintbrush

*Designer
Barbara Evans*

Bathing Beauty's Box

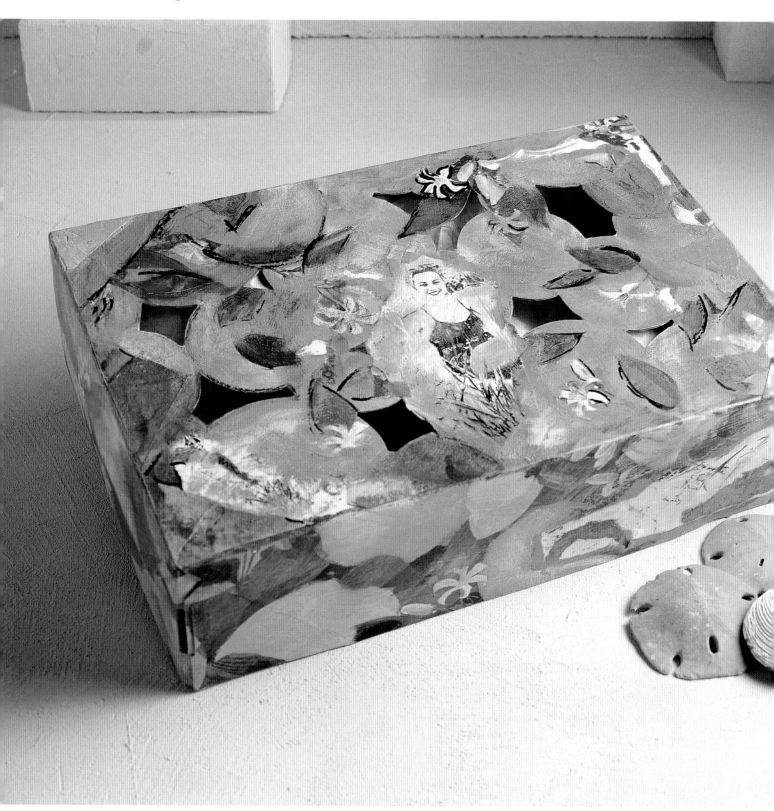

A COMMERCIAL BOX WITH PRECUT holes for the purpose of showing off colorful oranges was collaged with an old photo before it was enhanced with more paper collage and paint. The holes in the box make it a perfect gift box for silky gifts such as lingerie or a nightgown.

PROCESS

If you want to cut peepholes in the top of your box, outline them with a pencil, integrating them with the overall design. Use the mat knife to carefully saw the holes out of the box. If the edges of the holes are rough, use a small piece of sandpaper to smooth them.

Trim the photocopied image to fit the center of the box. Brush a coat of acrylic medium onto the center of the box, and press the photocopy into place. Smooth it out with your fingers to prevent bubbles. Brush another coat of acrylic medium on top of the image, and use the pressure of the brush to continue to smooth out the image. Allow the medium to dry.

Apply pieces of torn tissue paper randomly to the box with a brush and acrylic medium. Begin painting over the box's design with strokes of acrylic paint. Use the lines of the design as a guide for the placement of your paint strokes, or alter the design. Leave some areas of the printed design showing underneath. Add more paint and paper until you like the surface effect.

Allow the box to dry, and then apply a final coat or two of acrylic medium to the box to protect the surface.

Note: You can opt to use the dry adhesive method described on pages 22 through 24 to apply the collage components.

MATERIALS AND TOOLS

Commercial box printed with a design (such as an orange box or a gift box)

Pencil (optional)

Mat knife (optional)

Sandpaper (optional)

Photocopy of old photo

Scissors

Torn bits of tissue paper

Acrylic gloss medium

Acrylic paints that emulate the colors of the pattern on your box

Paintbrushes

Designer
Katherine Duncan Aimone

Table of Travels

MATERIALS AND TOOLS

Small, unfinished wooden table

Medium-grit sandpaper

Several colors of acrylic paint for background and edges of table

Paintbrushes

Collection of travel photos and other related print materials

Memorabilia such as game scorecards, ticket stubs, matchbooks, or menus

Small scissors and mat knife

Glue stick

Decorative cloth ribbon for legs (optional)

Rubber cement or fabric glue (optional)

Non-yellowing clear acrylic varnish

Designer
Tana H. Boerger

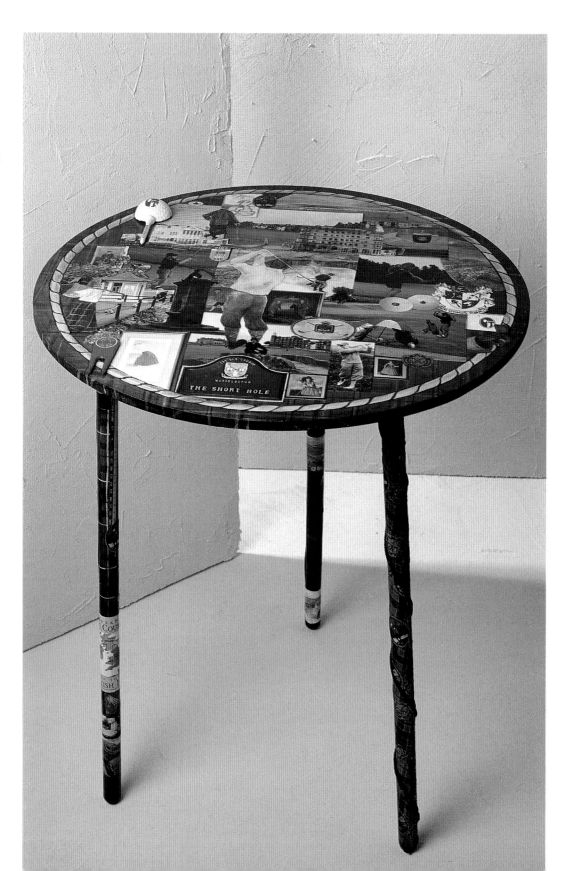

COLLECT PHOTOS FROM A TRIP, save them by making a collage on the top of a table, and you'll have a ready-made conversation piece! This designer took photos and memorabilia from a family golfing trip to St. Andrews in Scotland, and artfully compiled them into a colorful, puzzle-like composition.

PROCESS

Sand the top of the table to remove any rough spots. Paint the unfinished wood with a coat of colored acrylic paint that will serve as the background for the piece. (We used green to go with the golf photos.) Leave a margin around the outside edge of the table for adding a decorative border.

Assemble your collection of photos and memorabilia, and loosely arrange them on the tabletop or on your work surface until you discover an arrangement that you like.

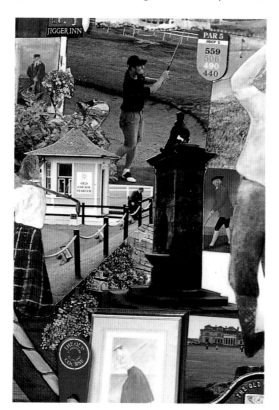

Trim each photo or image with small scissors and/or a mat knife, and begin to fit them together in a puzzle-like fashion. Overlap the edges of the photos as needed. (You can also cut out small portions of one photograph and superimpose those onto other photos.)

As you discover tight arrangements that you like, glue the photos into place with a glue stick. (Cover the back of each photo and the edges completely with glue so that the corners don't curl up later.) Continue to cover the table with photos and memorabilia until you've completed the composition.

Note: You can opt to use the dry adhesive method described on pages 22 through 24 to apply the collage components.

Paint a decorative border around the edge with acrylic paint. Use repeating squares, triangles, stripes, or other geometric components to create a pattern that complements your collage.

If the legs of your table are unfinished, you can decorate them with paint and patterned ribbon. Paint each leg with acrylic paint. After it dries, cut snippets of ribbon long enough to wrap around the circumference of each leg, and use rubber cement to glue them at intervals into place.

To seal the surface of the collage, brush on a coat or two of non-yellowing acrylic varnish. (This step is not necessary if you've used the dry adhesive method.)

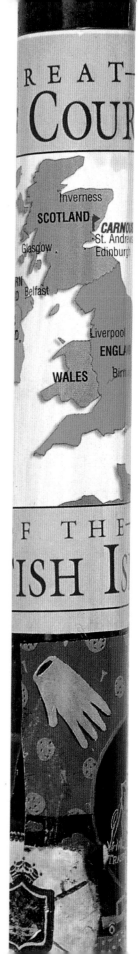

Artist's Paint Box

MATERIALS AND TOOLS

Cardboard box with shelves (former paper sample box from a print shop or box made to hold closet items from a home improvement store)

Sheets of construction paper or other heavy, colored paper cut into triangles of different sizes and colors

Found images from magazines cut into triangles

Acrylic matte medium

Acrylic paints

Paintbrushes

Medium-grit sandpaper

Designer
Katherine Duncan Aimone

THIS BOX WAS ORIGINALLY USED TO HOLD PAPER SAMPLES AT A PRINT SHOP. The paper samples were too beautiful and the box too intriguing to throw out, so both evolved into a painted and collaged unit to hold artist's supplies. If paint gets spilled or smeared on it, it just adds to the design!

PROCESS

Paint a coat of acrylic medium on the surface of the box to seal it and create a ground for applying paint and collage. Allow the medium to dry.

On one side of the box, begin applying triangles randomly by brushing the backs of them with acrylic medium, pressing them into place on the surface, and then painting over the top of them with more medium. Layer many triangles, building up the collage and the design as you go. Group triangles to form dense areas in your design, and leave other areas open.

Add strokes of acrylic paint to the background of the design and on top of the collaged pieces. Don't be afraid to cover up areas that you don't like.

To create variations in the design, rub away some of the acrylic paint so that stained pieces of paper are left. In certain areas, pull the still-moist paper off the surface to create the look of remnants. Continue adding to and taking away from the surface until you like what you see. Step back from the design and look for overall balance and interest in it. Add more triangles or paint to punctuate the design until it feels rhythmic as well as unified.

Paint the other sides of the box with the paints, and add a few bits of collaged paper as accents. Paint inside the shelves, and add collage papers as you wish.

Allow the surface to dry for about 30 minutes, or until slightly tacky. Sand the collaged surface lightly to create an abraded, weathered look. Add more touches of paint or collage at this point, or leave it as it is.

When you've completed this stage, paint the surface of the whole box with a couple of coats of acrylic medium to seal the collage.

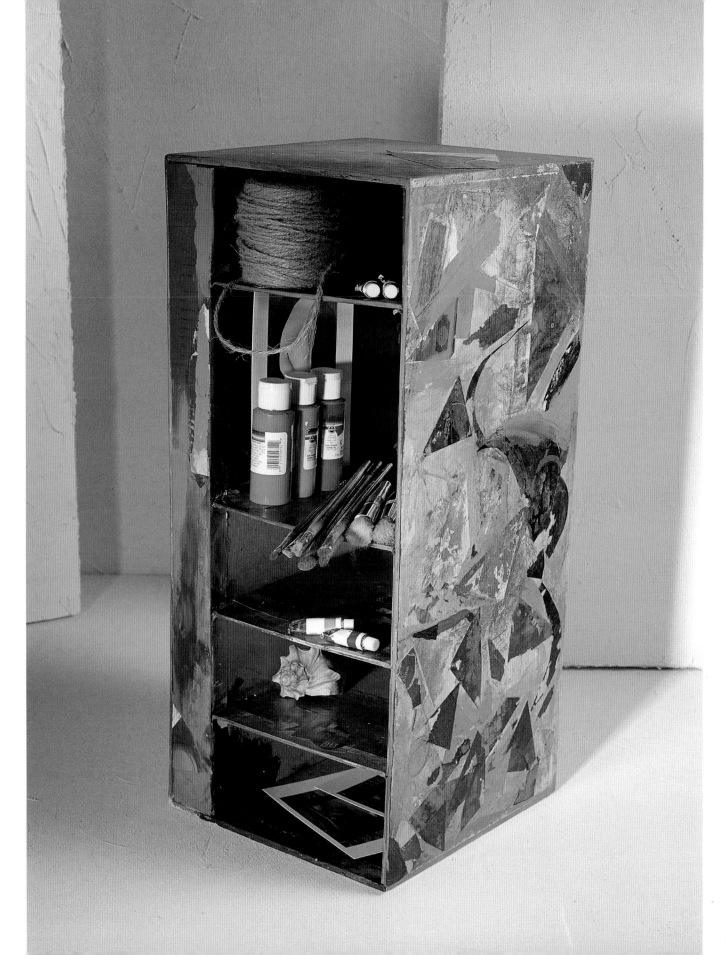

Wild, Wild West Wastebasket

MATERIALS AND TOOLS

Magazine clippings

Images cut from books given away by a local library

Craft knife or scissors

Acrylic matte medium

Paintbrush

Four-sided wooden wastebasket

Acrylic paints

Non-yellowing, clear, water-based polyurethane

Designer
Kathryn Semolic

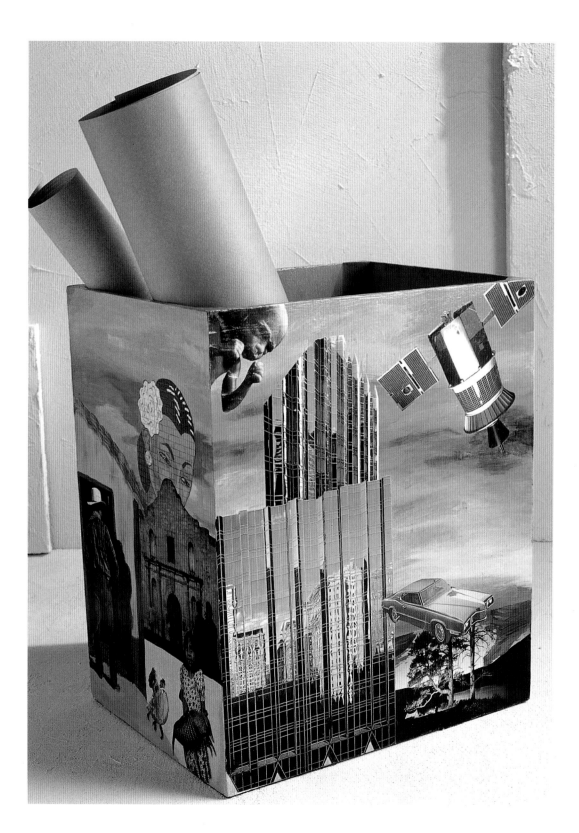

THE MURAL-LIKE COLLAGE THAT adorns the sides of this glorified wastebasket was created by the artist to express her love of the cultures and landscapes of Texas. She, like many other rugged individualists, was drawn to the wide open landscape of Texas.

Each side of the wastebasket depicts a different era and culture. A cowgirl under a full moon evokes the nostalgic vision of a life lived on the land. The independence of Texas won at the Alamo, the celebration of the state's Spanish and Mexican heritage, and technological advances that led to the rise of cities are also depicted. Texas archetypes such as the cowboy, the astronaut, and the oil tycoon are also included.

The last panel of the collage expresses the artist's concerns about the tension between the natural world and human technology, while indicating that there are means to rediscover individual connections to the universe. She feels that art is one of the ways in which we can become more aware.

I find the process of collage a lot like taking a vacation. I gather together what I think I'll need—always more than I actually use. Then I set off on my journey, peering at the images, comparing perspectives and moods. Gradually, a theme develops in my mind around several of the images. I explore further, taking little side trips, picking up unexpected items which often become central to my composition. I arrange the pieces, considering texture, tension, and tone. As I work, certain elements seem to fit naturally with others.

—*Kathryn Semolic*

PROCESS

Tear out pages from magazines and old books containing images that center around a theme of your choice (a portion of history, events of your own life, or a subject of interest). Cut out the images with a mat knife or scissors.

Use the paintbrush to apply a coat of acrylic matte medium to the sides of the box, and allow it to dry. (Doing this will seal the surface of the wood, and create a ground to paint on.)

Decide on the placement of the key images around the sides of the box. Brush a coat of acrylic medium on the back of each image, and press it into place around the sides. Add more images that relate to your theme to these key images. Build the composition on all sides by painting in blank areas with acrylic paint. Integrate the images with the painted areas.

After the paint and collage have completely dried, apply a coat of clear polyurethane to all sides of the wastebasket to protect your collage.

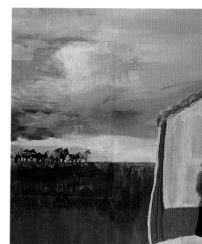

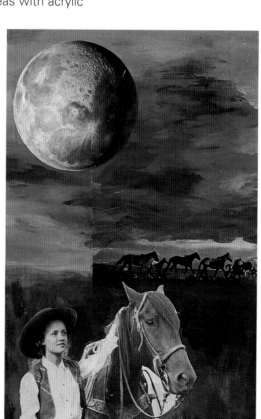

Exquisite Corpse Book

MATERIALS AND TOOLS

Assorted images of heads, legs, and torsos cut from magazines (Each sample should be approximately the same size. To adjust the size of an image, enlarge or reduce it on a photocopier.)

Scissors

Mat board

Mat knife

Ruler

Gesso

Paintbrushes

Pencil

Rubber cement

Acrylic matte medium

Coloring medium such as acrylic paints, watercolor pencils, or watercolor crayons

Awl

Electric drill with ¼-inch (6 mm) bit

2 covers cut from pieces of mat board or other heavy board for the cover

6 binder rings, ½ inch (1.3 mm) diameter

Designer
Amy Cook

THE PHRASE "THE EXQUISITE CORPSE" originated from a random word game played by the Surrealists (members of an art movement that developed around 1922).

Today, this term has been loosely adapted to books made with many images that can be recombined to create new ones by flipping pages divided into segments. This

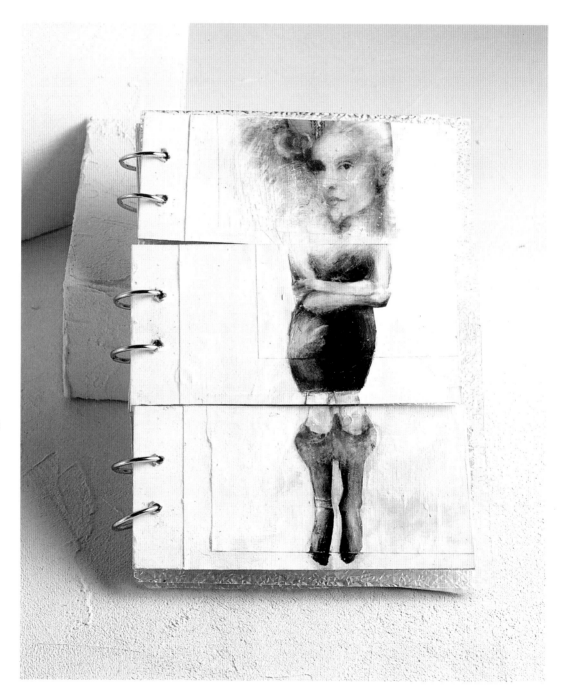

visual adaptation of the word game, which involves creating both bizarre and beautiful images of bodies, originated as an exercise to explore body image with teenage girls. Use collaged images from magazines or other sources to create your own exquisite corpse book.

PROCESS

Use the mat knife and ruler to cut several pieces of mat board to the same size (one for each page of your book). Prime the surface of the mat board by painting it with a coat of gesso to give it a smooth, uniform surface.

Decide on the height of each of the three sections that you'll be cutting to make sections for the book. Compare the proportions of the heads, torsos, and legs to determine this size. Each section (be it the top, middle, or bottom) must be the same size throughout the book so that you'll be able to flip the sections. Use a pencil and ruler to draw two dividing lines onto each board and divide it into three sections.

Lay out the sections of the boards a page at a time, and begin placing the cutout images on them. When you're satisfied with the placement, use rubber cement to adhere the images to the mat board. After the rubber cement dries, brush a coat of acrylic matte medium over the surface of each image to provide a smooth surface for painting and to protect the images. Allow the medium to dry. To unify the three sections of each of your pages, apply brushstrokes of acrylic paint to the overall image of each page. Use a style of painting that comes naturally to you. Allow the paint to dry.

Mark six equidistant points along the edge of one of the pages for the purposes of binding, and use the awl to poke holes at each of these points. Repeat this process with the other pages. Enlarge the holes with an electric drill outifitted with a ¼-inch (6 mm) bit, then cut each page into sections with the mat knife. Cut two pieces of mat board or other heavy board that are ⅛ inch (3 mm) wider than the book's pages on all sides. Drill corresponding binding holes in these two pieces of board.

Stack the pages between the covers in the position that you want them, and clip the binder rings into place.

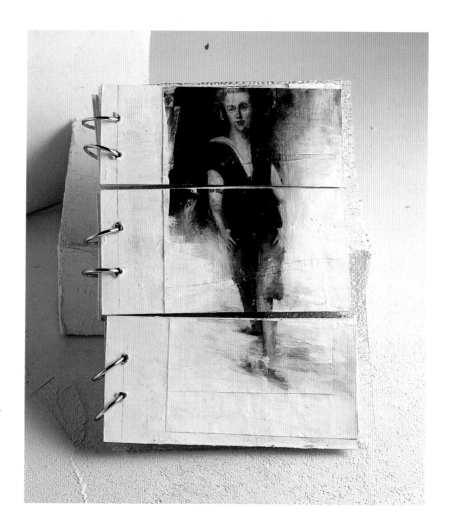

CD Collages

MATERIALS AND TOOLS

Old compact discs

Collage components such as magazine images, photographs, and rice paper

Small fingernail scissors and/or mat knife

Acrylic matte medium or white craft glue

Small paintbrush

Wallpaper seam roller

Baby wipes

Acrylic paint

Colored markers

Acrylic ground (for chalk pastels)

Chalk pastels

Spray fixative (for chalk pastels)

Designer
Carolyn Brooks

TRANSFORM THE SURFACE OF A COMPACT DISC that you might otherwise throw out into a piece of art. This artist collected images that held meaning for her, and combined them poetically with paint and pastel to create symbolic narratives. She worked on the pieces a bit at a time to allow new ideas and juxtapositions to emerge. Notice how her designs conform to the round shapes that contain them.

PROCESS

Gather colored images from magazines or photographs and think of a theme that you'd like to explore, or allow the theme to emerge as you create the piece.

Trim the images carefully with small scissors or a mat knife. Place them on the surface of one of the discs to see how they relate to one another. Move them around until you like the way that the images interact with one another. Apply each image carefully to the surface of the disc by brushing the back with a small amount of acrylic medium or white glue. Smooth out the papers with a narrow wallpaper seam roller. Wipe off the excess medium or glue with a baby wipe. Allow the collaged portions to dry completely.

Use paint, markers, and pastels to add color to the collage and surrounding background. When you use pastels, apply a coat of acrylic ground to the disc before applying them so that the chalk will stick. Use spray fixative on top of the pastel to keep it from smearing.

Collage can be deep or casual, spontaneous or transformed a hundred times, meticulous or delightfully imperfect. I paint with paper instead of always mixing paints—I usually find my colors, textures, and content in already existing papers and parts of images.

In working, collage becomes more of a dialogue between myself and the world, a response to what has already had a life in one form, has been rediscovered, and will now have a new life in a new form.

Collage has all the positive aspects of recycling with the additional component of creating unlikely juxtapositions of already existing images. It satisfies the hunter in me who needs a physical search to match the internal search.

—Carolyn Brooks

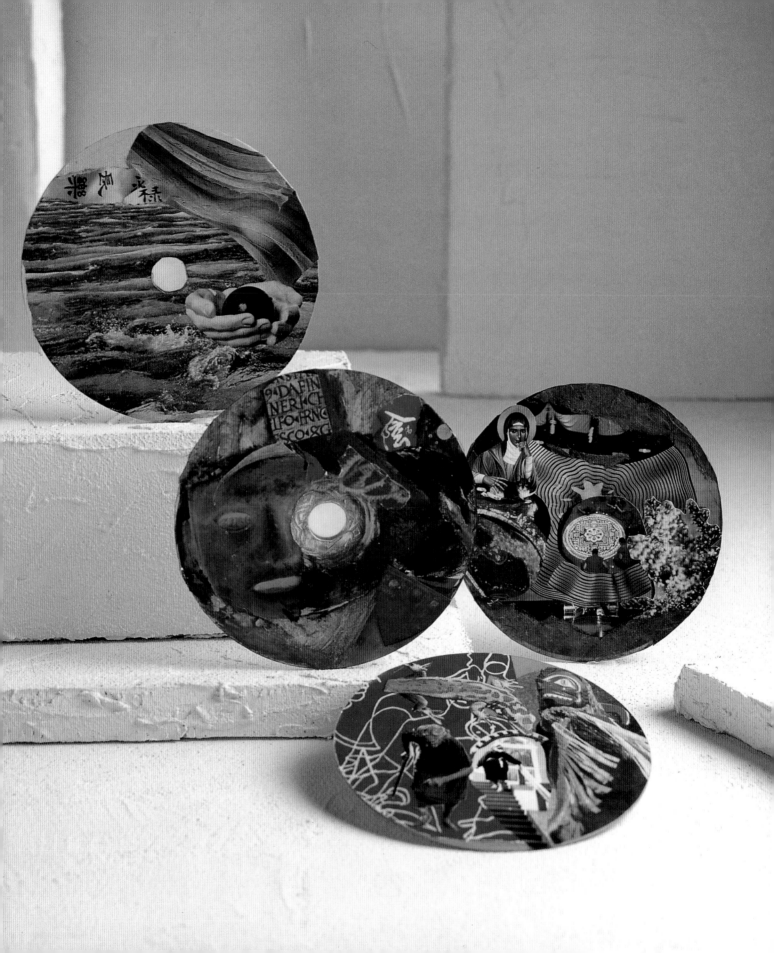

Collaged Triptych

MATERIALS AND TOOLS

Black mat board

Mat knife

Sheet of black paper

Scissors

Gel metallic pen in gold

Colorful, textured papers such as handmade papers, painted papers, Japanese papers, or rice papers

Metal ruler (optional)

White craft glue

Sewing machine

Gold metallic thread

Sewing needle

Small beads

Large embroidery needle

Black thread

Bamboo strips (optional)

Designer
Karen Page

THIS DESIGN COMBINES A VARIETY of media from the artist's studio that she keeps on hand all the time. Build your own stockpile of beautiful papers, beads, and threads, and you'll be inspired to make a triptych to give as as a special remembrance for someone close to you.

PROCESS

Cut out three rectangular pieces of mat board with the mat knife (the ones shown measure 9 x 6 inches [22.5 x 15 cm] each).

Trim the sheet of black paper to fit onto the board that you plan to place in the center of the triptych. Write a poem or message by hand in gold lettering on the paper.

Tear the edges of papers to fit onto the three boards (tear against the edge of a metal ruler if you want a clean edge). Glue the poem into the center of one of the pieces of paper.

Use a sewing machine to stitch lines of gold metallic thread onto the surfaces of the other two pieces of paper for embellishment. Use unusual stitches, and turn the papers to create curved lines. Sew small beads onto the papers to create visual interest.

Use craft glue to attach the three papers to the three pieces of mat board. Lay the pieces side by side to create a triptych formation. If you want, add other strips of paper or written messages to the collage with glue. Continue to embellish the piece until you're satisfied with the overall look of it.

Use a large embroidery needle to punch holes in the corners of the boards where you want to attach them to one another. Thread the needle with black thread, and sew the boards together to form hinges so that the triptych will fold. Leave end threads hanging, and add beads to them if you like. If you want to add a strip of bamboo to one end of the triptych for decoration, use the mat knife to trim the strip to roughly the height of the board. Punch holes in either end of the board where you want to attach the strip. Use a needle and thread to wrap and attach the strip to the board.

I work fast, I make my decisions rapidly, and I generate many pieces. I love to have about 15 projects going at the same time. Some are long term (a year or more), some take a couple of hours, and most are between the two extremes. When I have a stumbling block, I put the piece away and let the ideas simmer. Usually, in a week or a month the answers come. I don't agonize over my pieces. I don't believe that artists have to suffer. I consider creating to be an exciting, playful time—never work.

Most of my pieces are inspired by the materials I have on hand. I don't decide on a project and then go out and buy materials. I have paper, cloth, beads, paints, charms, pictures, threads, and yarn all around me on every flat surface. . .on the walls and on the floor. Something I see inspires me, and my next project begins. I never know what it will look like finished.

Once the ideas begin to pour in, one thing leads to another. I never anticipate what will happen. That is the joy of the creative process for me. Things are unexpected—there are surprises. The creative juices boil, the excitement builds, time becomes nonexistent, and a dialogue occurs. It's hard to explain. The process is everything. The product rarely has meaning for me.

—Karen Page

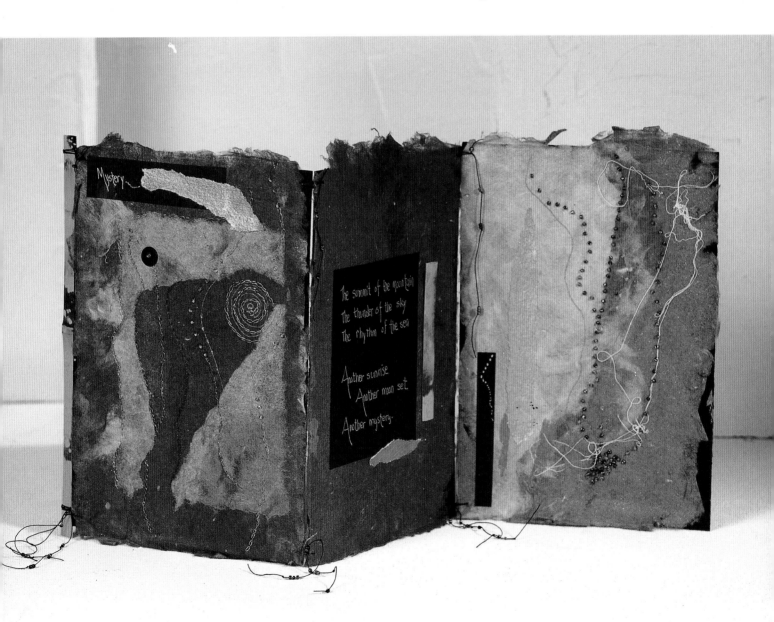

Polymer Clay Collage Pin

CREATE A BEAUTIFUL COLLAGED PIN from polymer clay and paper—even if you've never used polymer clay before, you'll be hooked once you try it.

MATERIALS AND TOOLS

Small block of white polymer clay

Small block of black polymer clay

Composition gold leaf (available at craft stores)

Acrylic rolling pin or pasta machine

Photocopy of pin design

Craft knife

Postage stamps or other paper collage elements

Items for stamping such as rubber stamps, lace, shells, charms, or beads

Acrylic paint

Paper towels

Pin back

CA glue (cyanoacrylate glue)

Lacquer finish glaze

Designer
Dayle Doroshow

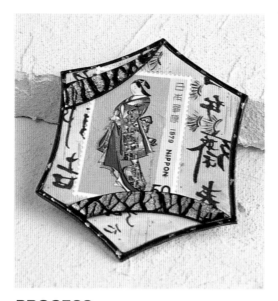

PROCESS

Plan the shape and design of your pin by drawing it out on a piece of paper, keeping in mind that the design will be reversed when you transfer it to the clay. Make a photocopy of the design.

Use an acrylic rolling pin or pasta machine to roll out a slab of white polymer clay to a ⅛-inch (3 mm) thickness. Roll the piece until it is slightly larger than your planned finished shape.

Place the photocopied design, toner side down, on top of the slab of clay. Burnish the back of the paper gently with your fingers to make sure there are no air bubbles and to ensure good contact between the toner and the clay. After letting the slab sit

for 30 minutes, peel the paper off slowly to reveal the shape. Cut out the pin with the craft knife. Position the postage stamp or other paper component on the clay to see how it will fit into your design.

To add polymer clay components with a gold leaf crackle, roll out a small sheet of black clay to a ⅛-inch (3 mm) thickness. Lay composition gold leaf on top of the clay, and burnish it with your fingers. Stretch the clay slightly with your fingers, or roll it with the roller to make the leaf crackle. Cut out shapes from this clay that you want to layer onto the pin. Layer them over the stamp or paper component to see how they look. Roll out a very narrow band of gold leaf clay, and press it into place around the edge of the pin if you want a border. Add texture to the surface of the pin by pressing it with rubber stamps or objects of your choice.

Remove the gold leaf pieces and the stamp or paper from the pin. Bake the pin and other polymer clay pieces according to the clay manufacturer's directions in a conventional oven. Allow them to cool. Rub in brown acrylic paint (or color of your choice) to highlight the stamped surface of the pin. Rub off the excess paint with a damp paper towel.

Glue the stamp or paper components onto the pin as well as the gold leaf pieces. Brush a coat of lacquer finish glaze onto the pin to protect the paper and gold leaf. Glue the back on the pin.

Rococo Basket

THIS BASKET, COVERED WITH FEATHERY wisps of tissue paper, is for those who love ornamentation and frills.

PROCESS

If you don't find a pre-made paper basket form that you like, you can make your own from a lightweight cardboard gift box. Open out the top flaps of the box and cut them off with the craft knife. Then draw curved lines at the top of each side of the box to be cut into curved flaps. Cut these with scissors or a craft knife. Push them out slightly so that they bow out.

Tear pieces of patterned and colored tissue paper into small pieces. Beginning at the top of the box beneath the flap, glue a loose row of pieces into place around the periphery of the box with decoupage glue or craft glue. (Glue the paper pieces so that the tops of them point to the top of the basket and the bottoms are secured.) Glue another row of paper pieces next to this line so that the papers overlap. (The designer compares this process to adding shingles to a roof.) In the process of gluing on the papers, glue on snippets of thread and yarn that are allowed to dangle. Continue adding rows of "feathers" until you reach the bottom of the box. The papers will fluff up and out like feathers.

Glue a border of lace around the edge of the bottom of the box. At the top of the box, use thick glue to add a collage of patterned paper, paint, charms, and trinkets.

Use glue and the paintbrush to collage the inside of the basket with layered strips of torn tissue paper. Use the gold pen to coat the top edge of the basket with gold ink, and add highlights to other parts of the basket as you wish.

MATERIALS AND TOOLS

Paper basket (make your own or buy one)

Craft knife (optional)

Scissors

Patterned and colored tissue paper

Lace

Yarn and metallic threads

Decoupage glue or white craft glue

Paintbrush

Pen with gold ink

Found objects such as charms, trinkets, and strips of webbing

Thick, tacky glue

Designer
Kathy Anderson

Metalscape Coat Rack

MATERIALS AND TOOLS

7 x 24 inch (17.5 x 60 cm) piece of luan plywood

Black paint (acrylic latex or enamel)

Pencil

Metal sheers

Scraps of copper, brass, and aluminum sheeting (from a home improvement store, junk store, or machine shop)

Pieces of screen and mesh in a variety of gauges and metals (from a home improvement store)

Black fine-tipped marker

Brass, copper, and black carpet tacks

Small hammer

Medium-sized nail

Piece of scrap wood

1 x 24 inch (2.5 x 60 cm) strip of oak

Wood glue

4 or 5 brass coat hooks

1¼ inch (3 cm) screws

Electric handheld screwdriver

Tip: Look in the bins that you find at a home improvement store that contain metal sheeting cut into shapes made for electrical work, plumbing, or other uses to find readymade metal shapes.

Designer
Cori Saraceni

A LOVE OF THE TEXTURES FOUND IN A variety of metals continue to inspire this artist to create unusual pieces. By composing a design made up of metal sheeting and screening, she converted this coat rack into a stylish, contemporary objet d'art.

PROCESS

Paint the piece of plywood with a coat of black paint. Allow it to dry completely. Use a pencil to mark off a 1 inch (2.5 cm) margin on one side of the wood for placement of the oak strip later.

Use the metal sheers to cut the scraps of metal sheeting into a variety of shapes, or use them as they are. Begin placing them on the black painted board several inches above the line you drew earlier. Play with the design until you have an idea of the placement of the first layer of pieces.

Use the metal sheers to cut pieces of screen and mesh that can be layered on top of these shapes. Play with the arrangement of these pieces on top of the first layer. Overlap and contrast metals, allowing them to show through the mesh and screen.

When you've arrived at a composition that you like, use the fine-tipped marker to make dots on the metal shapes that indicate key places to attach them to the wood. Place the metal pieces on a piece of scrap wood, and use the nail and the hammer to puncture holes into the metal.

Place the pieces back on the plywood, and attach them lightly to the plywood with carpet tacks and the small hammer. Add the next layer of screening and other shapes, and attach these with tacks as well. (Make the carpet tacks a part of the finished design as much as possible.) Con-

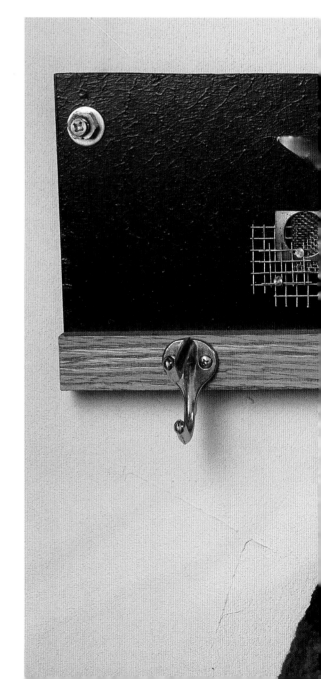

tinue to add pieces of metal until you are satisfied with the design.

Glue the strip of oak along the bottom edge of the board. Allow it to dry completely. Use the electric screwdriver to mount the brass coat hooks into place at even intervals along the oak strip.

Contrasting materials have always piqued my creativity. Because of this, I chose to use light fencing and metal screens in this piece to permit simultaneous viewing of surfaces that have been layered. The composition is built upon steps that lead the viewer's eyes from left to right to center to either side again—in an attempt to keep the viewer's interest.

—*Cori Saraceni*

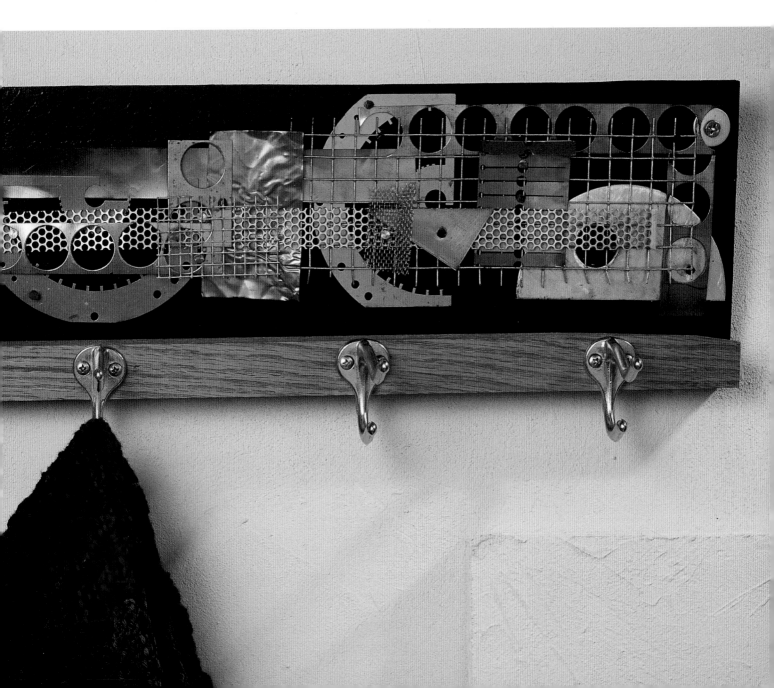

Box Basket

MATERIALS AND TOOLS

Cardboard box or papier-mâché box from a craft store

Mat knife (optional)

Scissors

Marbled papers

Papyrus paper or other textured paper

Dried leaves

Leaf skeletons (find them outside on the ground or buy simulated ones at a craft store)

Gold leaf

White craft glue or acrylic matte medium

Sponge brush

Matte lacquer spray

¼-inch (6 mm) flat black ribbon

Thick, tacky glue

Awl

Black wax linen thread, embroidery thread, or carpet thread

Large-eyed embroidery needle

Mat board

Old newspapers

Black spray paint

Designer
Diane Peterson

THIS DESIGNER TRANSFORMED A small, rectangular cardboard box into a gorgeous home accessory.

PROCESS

If you're using a cardboard box, cut away the flaps with the mat knife to leave straight edges around the top.

Use the sponge brush and a solution of glue or acrylic medium and water to collage the surface of the box with an array of marbled papers, textured papers, dried leaves, leaf skeletons, and gold leaf. Layer the components randomly and diagonally. Allow the collage to dry.

In a well-ventilated room or outside, spray the surface with a coat of matte lacquer spray to seal and protect it. Use thick, tacky glue to add a ¼-inch (6 mm) flat ribbon around the top edge of the box. Allow the glue to dry.

Punch evenly-spaced holes with the awl around the top edge of the basket underneath the ribbon border. Thread the needle with heavy black thread, and lace it through the holes to create a finished edge.

Cut a strip of mat board wide enough and long enough to serve as a handle for your basket. Place the strip outside on newspapers, and spray it with a coat of black spray paint on both sides. Allow the board to dry, then gradually bend it into the shape of a handle. (Be careful not to crease it when you do this.) Attach the handle to the inside of the basket with thick, tacky glue. Allow the glue to set before touching the handle.

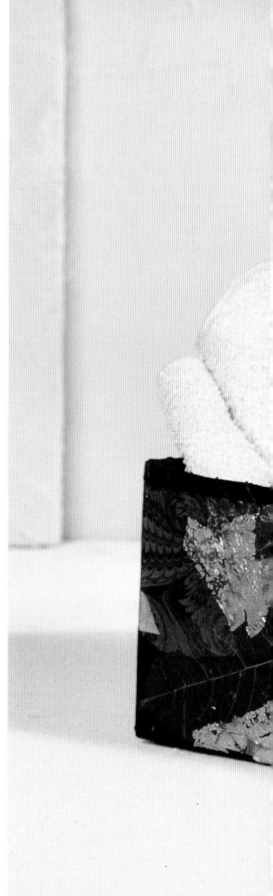

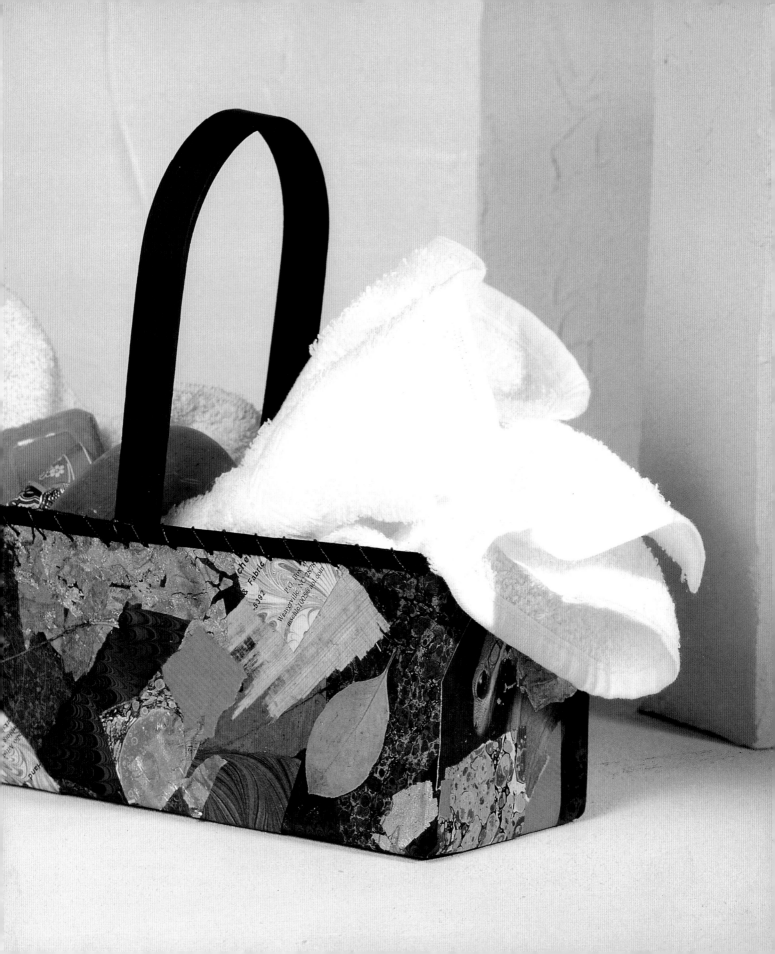

Frayed Fabric Collage

MATERIALS AND TOOLS

Fabrics for layering, such as pieces of old, worn clothing; natural fibers such as cotton, linen, silk, and wool; fabrics with loose weaves such as tabby or twill; nylon netting

White craft glue or fabric glue

Sewing machine with darning foot

Sewing needle

Thread

Found objects such as bones, vintage buttons, beads, shells, small dolls, and figurines

Mat board

Frame with glass removed

Designer
Luann Udell

THIS DESIGNER CREATED this beautiful fabric collage by combining her own techniques with some learned from other artists. The polymer clay horses (that she calls artifacts) were inspired by Tory Hughes's method for making "faux ivory" polymer clay pieces. She modified this idea to imitate the look of fossilized bone and ivory. (Substitute real objects such as bones and charms to make a similar collage.) She credits fabric artist Susan Carlson for her introduction to the layered fiber collage technique that was used to make this piece.

PROCESS

Collect fabric swatches with texture and a wide weave (see suggestions above). Cut the fabrics into pieces for the purpose of layering and machine quilting them. Ravel the edges by pulling threads from the weave.

Use one piece of fabric as the base for your collage. Place the others on top as you wish them to be, and then use small dots of glue to hold them in place on top of one another. Allow the glue to dry thoroughly.

Equip your sewing machine with a darning foot and thread. Drop the feed dogs on the machine down so that you will be able to push and pull the material by hand.

Overstitch the fabric with a straight stitch sewn in an organic pattern. Push and pull the material around in circles, back and forth, and sideways as needed. When you're sewing in this manner, you'll control the stitch length with how fast you move the material and how hard you push the foot pedal. Sew over the frayed edges of the fabrics as you sew, or leave them hanging.

After you've finished overstitching, use a needle and thread to sew found objects into place on the surface by hand (you can also glue them into place).

Cut a piece of mat board that fits your frame, and mount the collage on the board with rubber cement so that the edges are covered once you put the frame into place. Pop the collage into the frame (with the glass removed), and close the back.

My aesthetic is to create something that looks like an ancient textile fragment, perhaps something recovered from an archeological site, or something that has been preserved and treasured in a clan for thousands of years. I want it to look frayed and unraveled, and showing evidence of having been repaired many, many times, by expert and not-so-expert hands.

So, when I stitch, I create patterns that, in my mind, resemble organic, intricate surfaces such as lichen or moss. Sometimes I use jagged lines and zig-zags, as if I were darning the fabric. Other times I sew some edges down so firmly that they merge into the underlying fabric. Or I might pull a section loose and actually shred the fibers.

—Luann Udell

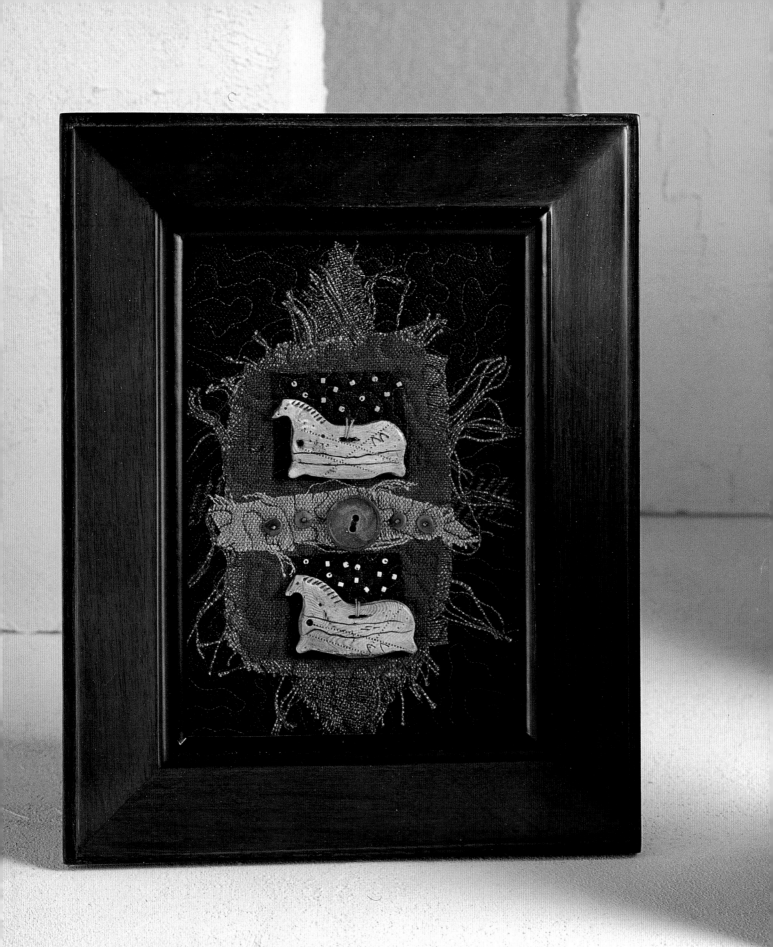

Dresser Tray

MATERIALS AND TOOLS

Assortment of papers (machine milled and handmade) in a variety of textures, colors, patterns, and weights

Dried leaf skeletons (from nature or a craft store)

Scissors

Mat knife

Metal ruler

Rubber cement

Wooden food skewer or toothpick

Large-eyed needle

Gold metallic thread

Waxed linen threads (used for bookbinding) or embroidery threads in colors that complement the papers

Small, hand-held drill

Panoramic style wooden frame

Drawer pulls

Four framing spacers (from frame shop)

Heavy paper

Spraymount

Four beads to be used as feet for the tray

Glue gun or thick, tacky glue

Designer
Kim Tibbals-Thompson

THIS ELEGANT TRAY THAT'S PERFECT for holding men's cuff links or coins is made from a simple wooden frame embellished with drawer pulls for handles.

PROCESS

Assemble papers and leaf skeletons that you want to layer to make a collage that will fit into your frame. Cut them with scissors or a craft knife. Use the metal ruler to tear and soften some of the paper edges. Layer them in a pattern of your choice, and glue them into place with rubber cement.

To create dimension, roll the end of one of the pieces of paper around a wooden skewer or toothpick, tuck the edge underneath, and glue the paper into place on the collage. Thread the needle with gold metallic thread, and lace the thread through the paper and over the skewer or toothpick. Continue this process until you've covered the stick with gold lacing.

Bunch waxed linen or embroidery threads, and swirl them on top of your design. Tack them in place with gold thread sewn through the paper.

Use the hand drill to bore holes in either end of the frame. Attach the drawer pulls to the frame through the holes.

When you're satisfied with your design, apply the spacers to the edges of the glass inside the frame to create a shallow area for your collage. Place the collage in the frame underneath the spacers. Seal the back of the frame with a piece of heavy paper cut to size and spray adhesive. Use the glue gun or tacky glue to attach four beads to the corners of the tray's back to serve as feet for the tray.

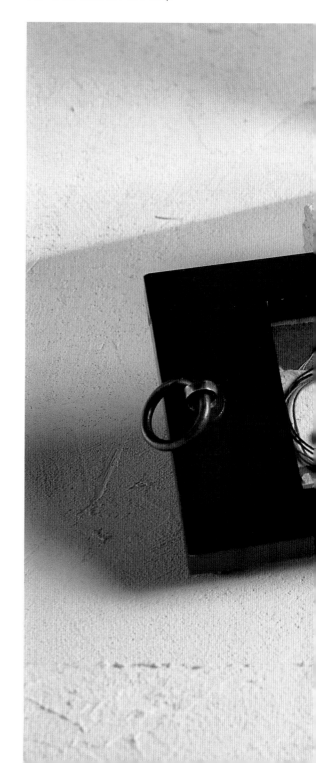

What I enjoy the most about collage is that no matter how hard you work at the planning stage, the part that makes it all work happens when you let go of the plan. While a basic structure is necessary to give the design a strong foundation, remaining open to the opportunities that present themselves as you work is what makes collage exciting to me. The trick is in recognizing those opportunities and being willing to move with them.

—Kim Tibbals-Thompson

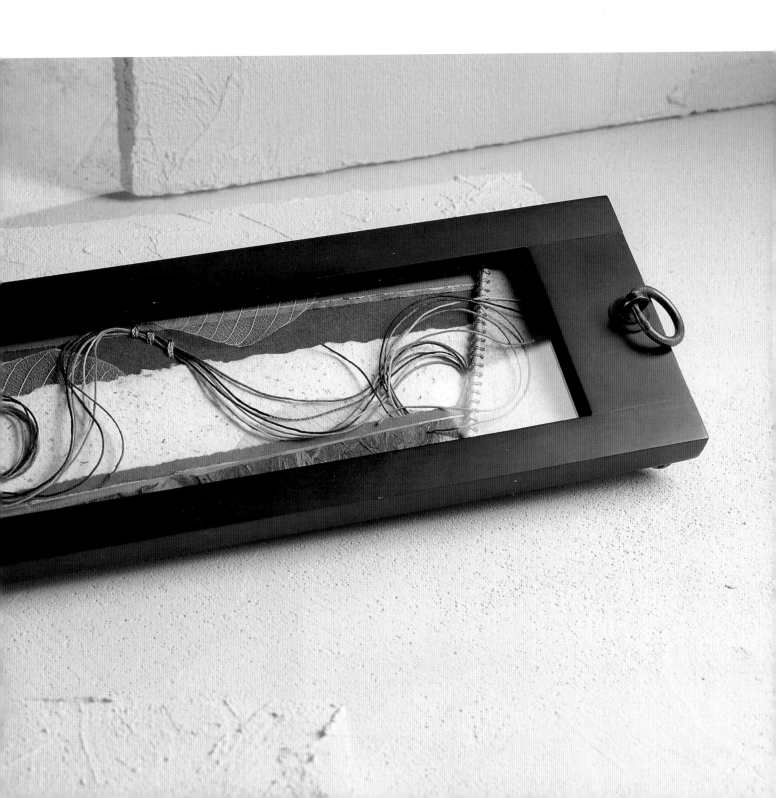

Scarf & Accessory Box

MATERIALS AND TOOLS

Wooden box with sliding top

Acrylic paints in several colors to use for blending

Sponge

Magazine and newspaper clippings

Decoupage glue or acrylic medium

Foam brush or paintbrush

Crumpled pieces of foil

Pieces of yarn and metallic thread

Found objects such as feathers, canceled postage stamps, charms, beads, thumbtacks

Wax-based metallic finish for antiquing

Soft rubbing cloth

Thick, tacky glue

Rubber stamps and stamp pad

Rubber brayer with mesh design

Two strips of bamboo

Copper wire

Designer
Kathy Anderson

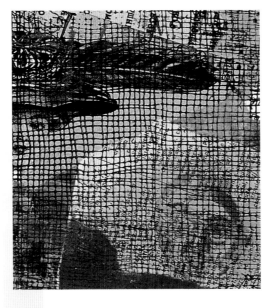

EVERY AVAILABLE BIT OF SURFACE ON this wooden box is embellished with an interesting, detailed collage. The designer used layers of unusual materials and techniques to keep the viewer engaged at every turn.

PROCESS

To create a colored background for the collage components, lightly sponge areas of color next to one another on the box, blending together the edges where the colors meet as you go. Allow the paint to dry.

Cut out images from magazines and newspapers, and collage them on top of the painted background with glue or acrylic medium. Overlap and smooth them with your fingers as you go.

On top of this layer of collage, add components such as crumpled pieces of foil, metallic thread, and found objects such as charms, feathers, and thumbtacks. If objects are heavy, use the thick, tacky glue to attach them.

Use the rubber stamps and stamp pad to add more designs to your collaged surfaces. As a final touch, roll the mesh-embossed brayer through acrylic paint, and add this texture to the surface of the box. After the paint and glue dry, rub the whole box with a wax-based metallic finish to give it an antique look. Rub away the excess finish with a clean cloth.

To serve as a handle for pulling the box open, cut a couple of strips of bamboo, wrap them loosely with copper wire, and attach them to the top of the box with tacky glue.

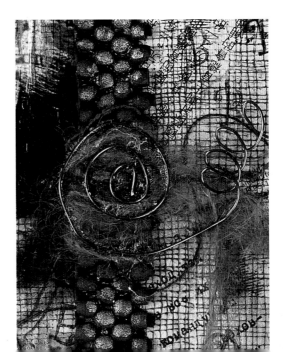

The process of collage allows me to create as I go. I love the way it opens my mind to all sorts of art processes that I can do without there being a right or wrong way.

I still keep composition in mind when I'm working, and try to draw on a theme or a focal point. I first see the design in my head and then translate it to the piece, very rarely drawing it out first. I make it look like what I see in my mind.

The colors, papers, and oddities are endless, and it's fun to collect and make something out of what others consider useless objects. I even save dryer lint! It's easier for me to find a theme with collage than with any other art form. The ideas and pictures come to me more easily. This form of art makes me feel loose, free, and unencumbered.

—Kathy Anderson

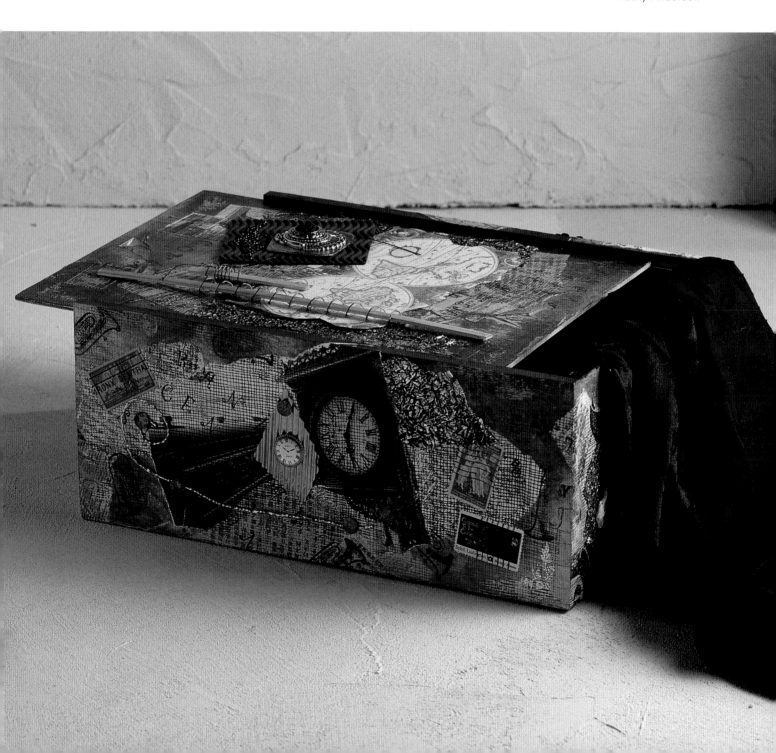

Snack Time Lunch Box

MATERIALS AND TOOLS

Old lunch box

Found images from magazines or books

Scissors

Acrylic matte medium

Paintbrush

Pencil

Acylic paint

Designer
Lynn Whipple

THIS ARTIST COLLECTS OLD PHOTOS and books as sources for images in her collage work, and enjoys playing with unlikely combinations and juxtapositions. This red plaid lunch box reminded her of childhood, and she couldn't resist making it into a collaged and painted piece.

Inspired by a classic picture found in an old cookbook of a boy eating a sandwich, she was on her way to transforming her vintage box. By using cleverly placed lines and paint, she altered the image and created a hat and shoulders for the boy from the plaid background. She added paint and another found image to the thermos to complete the humorous set.

PROCESS

Find an old lunch box that you like at a thrift store or garage sale. Clean it up with soap and water if it is dirty. Find an illustration from an old cookbook or magazine for the front of the box. Cut out and crop the image with clean edges. Brush a coat of acrylic matte medium over the front of the box to create a good surface for applying paint, and allow it to dry.

Brush the back of your image with medium, and apply it to the box, leaving a margin around it so that you can play with the pattern of the background.

Use a pencil to extend the lines of your image anywhere that you've cropped it, so that the pattern on the box becomes a part of the image. Wash the acrylic medium from your brush, and apply a coat of paint outside of the lines that you've drawn to form a background for the image.

Clip out an image or word that complements the composition you've created, and use the same process to apply a collage and paint to the thermos.

Putting together images that might never be seen together makes the process of collage fun. It also keeps your studio looking like a pile of papers! You constantly have to sort and sift, trying dozens of things before the perfect combination strikes your eye, and hopefully your sense of humor.

—Lynn Whipple

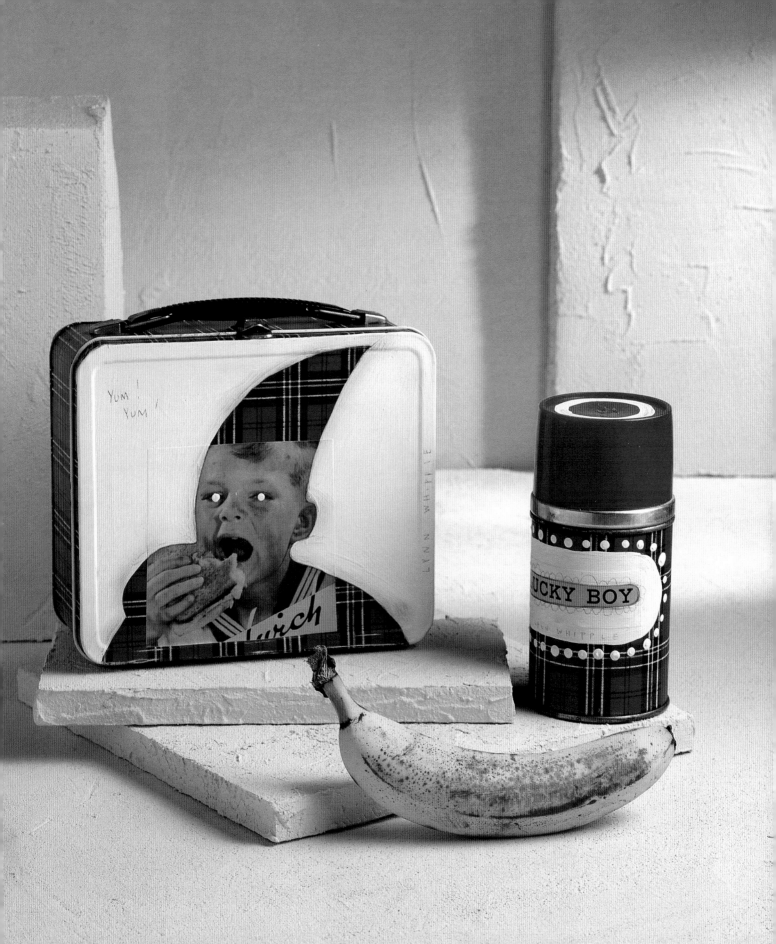

Two of Hearts Vase

MATERIALS AND TOOLS

Cylindrical cardboard vase

Sheets of corrugated paper in several colors of your choice

Pencil

Ruler

Scissors

Thick, tacky glue

Paintbrush

Deck of playing cards

Small objects such as plastic beads, sequins, trinkets, costume jewels

Dark-colored acrylic paint

Tall glass or vase that is smaller in diameter than the cardboard vase

Designer
Pat Samuels

THE DESIGNER USED BRIGHT COLORS and repeating patterns to create this jazzy vase. By cutting playing cards into pieces and reassembling them, she found a new use for old motifs.

PROCESS

Decide on a basic geometric design for covering the cardboard vase with pieces of corrugated paper. Draw lines on the back of the paper with the ruler to indicate where you want to cut the paper, and cut out pieces to begin the process of cover-

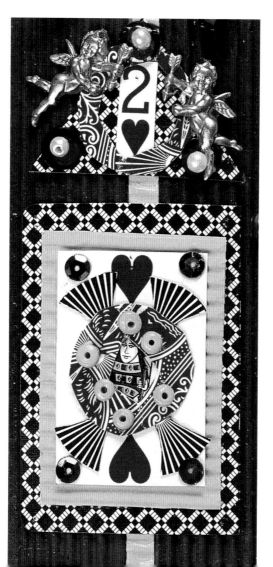

ing the vase. (For variety in the finished piece, cut some pieces with vertical corrugations, and others with horizontal ones.)

Spread tacky glue with the brush on the back of the corrugated pieces, and press them into place in a puzzle-like fashion on the vase's surface to create a pattern of contrasts between color and shape.

When you've finished covering the vase, cut out shapes from the playing cards that can be layered with shapes cut from corrugated paper to create medallions to be added to the vase. For instance, this designer layered a rectangular piece of a card, a smaller rectangle of cardboard, another piece from a card showing the face of a king or queen, and a combination of doughnut-shaped and fan-shaped cutouts from cards. She allowed the faces of the king and queen cards to show through the holes in the center of the doughnut-shaped pieces.

After you've layered the cards and corrugated cardboard to make designs, glue small objects such as plastic beads, sequins, trinkets, and costume jewels on top of the layered papers at points that fit your design. Glue on other beads and adornments to the surface of the vase to create an overall pattern.

After you've finished, paint the inside of the vase with a dark shade of acrylic paint. Fill the tall glass or vase with water, and drop it into the cardboard vase to hold your favorite flowers.

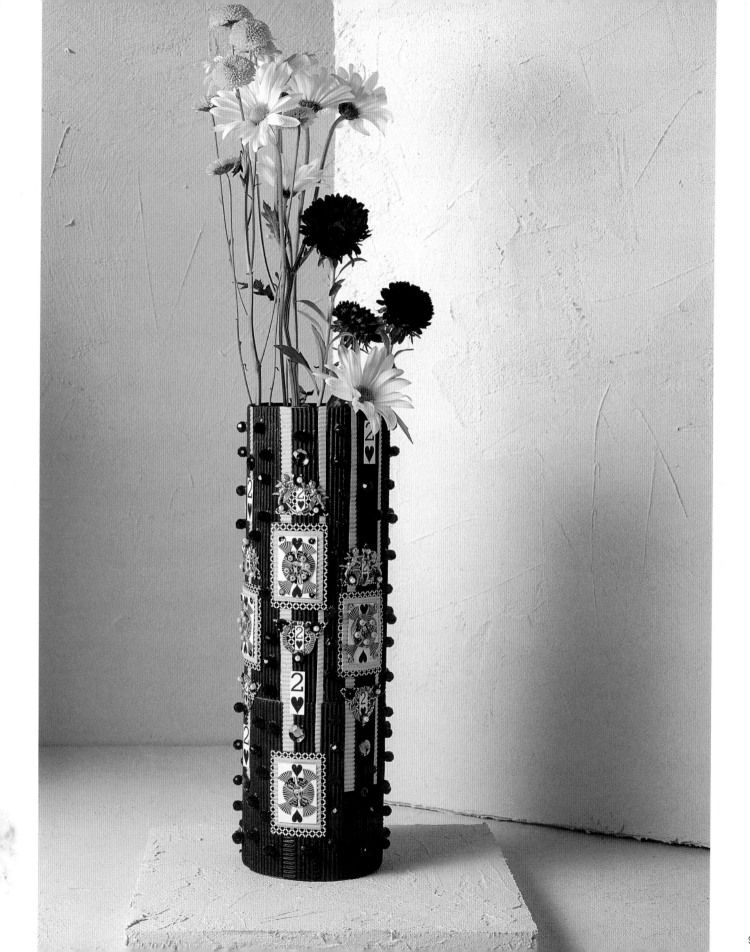

Chinatown Boxes

MATERIALS AND TOOLS

Images from an old encyclopedia or other source

Tissue paper

Tissue paper printed with Chinese lettering or other interesting pattern

Magazine clippings

Scissors

Papier-mâché boxes

Rubber cement

Paintbrush

Matte varnish

Designer
Megan Kirby

THE DESIGNER CLIPPED IMAGES from an old encyclopedia that she found at a thrift shop to use as focal points for this beautiful set of boxes covered with Chinese papers. She says that she enjoys the process of taking images out of their original context and placing them in new ones to create different meanings.

PROCESS

Cut out images from an old book or a magazine to use as focal points for your collaged boxes. Use scissors to cut out rectangular pieces of colored tissue paper and patterned paper that fit the sections of the boxes.

Paint a coat of rubber cement on the lid of one of the boxes, and begin placing the tissue paper and patterned paper on the boxes in a design of your choice. Smooth out the pieces as you go. Lap the edges of the paper underneath the edges of the lid to create a smooth edge. Continue this process to cover the bottom of the box with a layer of the same tissue and patterned papers.

Position the book and magazine images that you cut out earlier on the tops of the boxes and brush rubber cement on the back of each before gluing them into place. Allow the rubber cement to dry, and brush on a coat of matte varnish to seal the surface of the boxes.

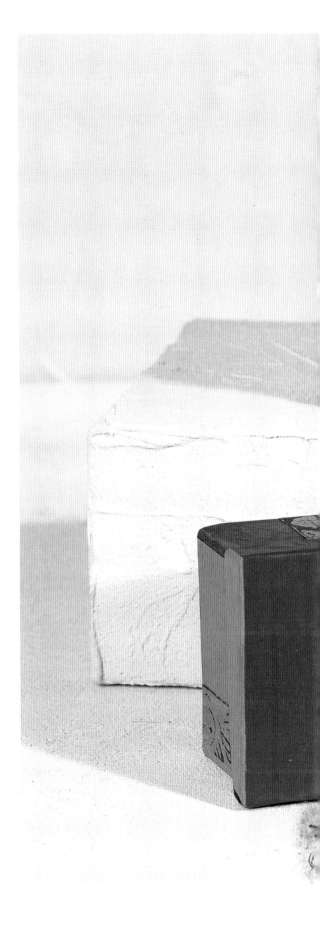

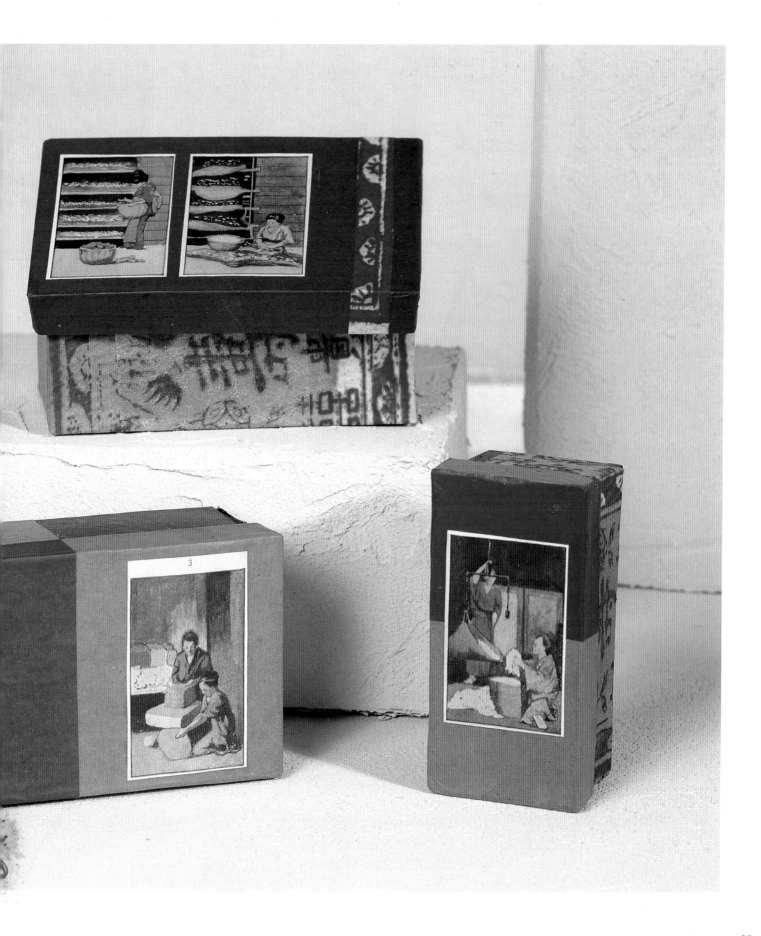

Reflective Mirrors

MATERIALS AND TOOLS

Hand mirror with a flat back

Found papers and magazine clippings

Papers colored with paint, ink, or colored pencils

Rice paper

Small fingernail scissors or mat knife

Acrylic matte medium, or white craft glue

Paintbrushes

Acrylic paint

Colored markers

Wax paper or brown kraft paper

Wooden wallpaper seam roller

Baby wipes

Designer
Carolyn Brooks

THESE EXQUISITE COLLAGED HAND mirrors provide an excuse to stop and contemplate surfaces filled with texture, color, and intriguing detail. The artist says that she "likes the idea of collaging a common object to reflect the importance of art as an everyday part of life."

PROCESS

Tear out pages from magazines and collect papers that relate to one another in color, design, and theme. Cut out shapes from magazines to fill the background of the mirror's back.

Place the mirror on a work surface covered with wax paper or brown kraft paper. Brush acrylic matte medium or white craft glue onto the back of the mirror, and begin pressing the papers into place. Roll out air bubbles with the wallpaper seam roller. Use baby wipes to remove the excess glue.

Add swatches of paper that you've colored with artists' media such as paint or colored pencils. Continue to add to your design, filling the back of the mirror with layers of images and color.

Use acrylic paint to color areas between images, and alter the images as you wish. (Gold paint can be used to enhance the handle of the mirror.) Allow the collage to dry, and then apply a coat of acrylic medium on top to seal the surface.

Note: You can opt to use the dry adhesive method described on pages 22 through 24 to apply the collage components.

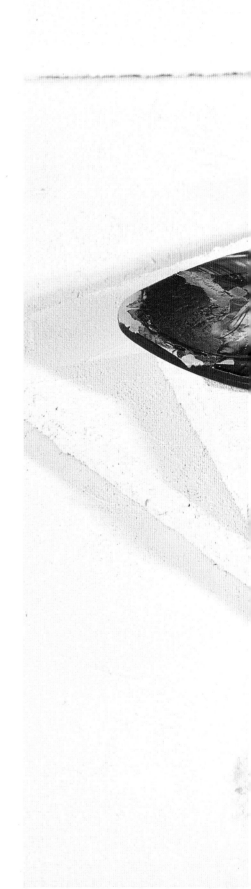

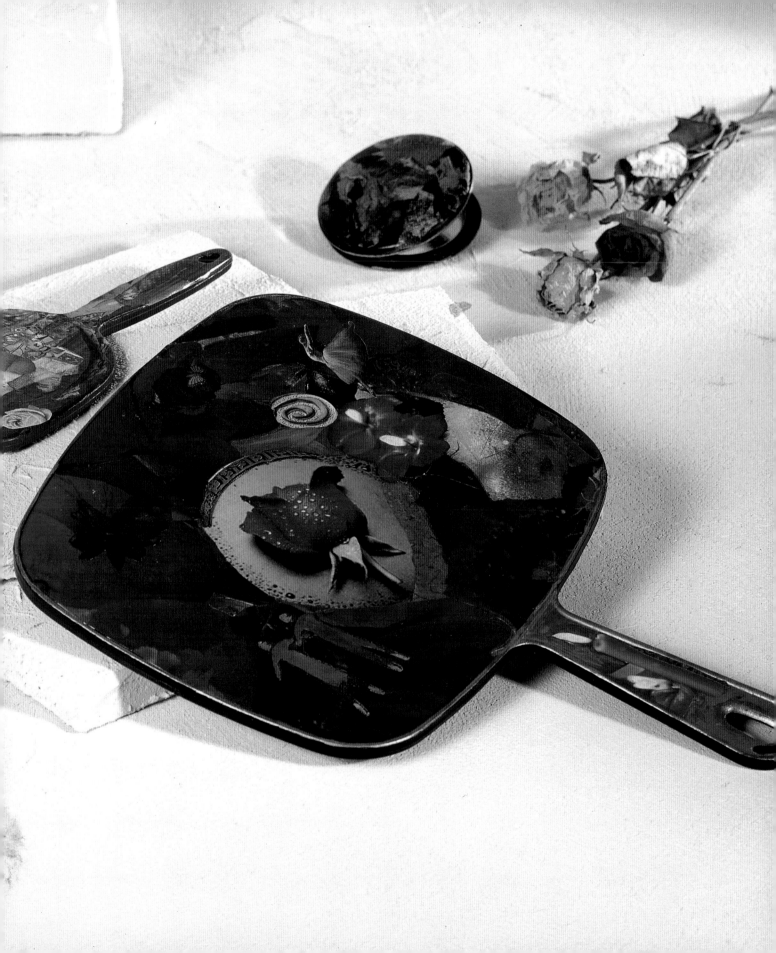

Good Fortune Vest

MATERIALS AND TOOLS

Sewing pattern for vest

Black fiberglass window screen (from the hardware store)

Sewing pins

Scissors

Black sewing thread

Sewing machine

Needle and thread

Collection of collage components such as small objects, fortune cookie messages, fabric scraps, photographs, fragments of letters, pins, buttons, beads, small drawings, gumball machine rings, ribbon, rickrack braid, ticket stubs, small stones

Designer
Mary D'Alton

BOXES FULL OF PHOTOS and other trinkets that this designer kept because they evoked memories were sewn onto this unusual vest made out of window screen. She enjoyed taking a collection of disparate pieces and joining them to create something joyous and colorful.

PROCESS

Choose a pattern for a vest, and lay out the pieces of it on a sheet of black window screen. Pin the pieces to the screen, and cut them out with scissors as you would fabric. Thread the sewing machine with black thread, and stitch together the shoulder seams and side seams.

Sew your saved fabric scraps, trinkets, and other treasures onto the screen with a needle and thread. Layer the components until you are satisfied with the design. (This vest is organized by placing the warm colored pieces on the front and the cool colored pieces on the back.)

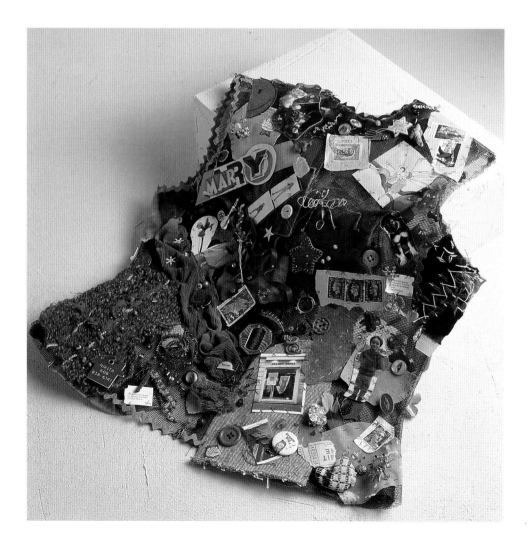

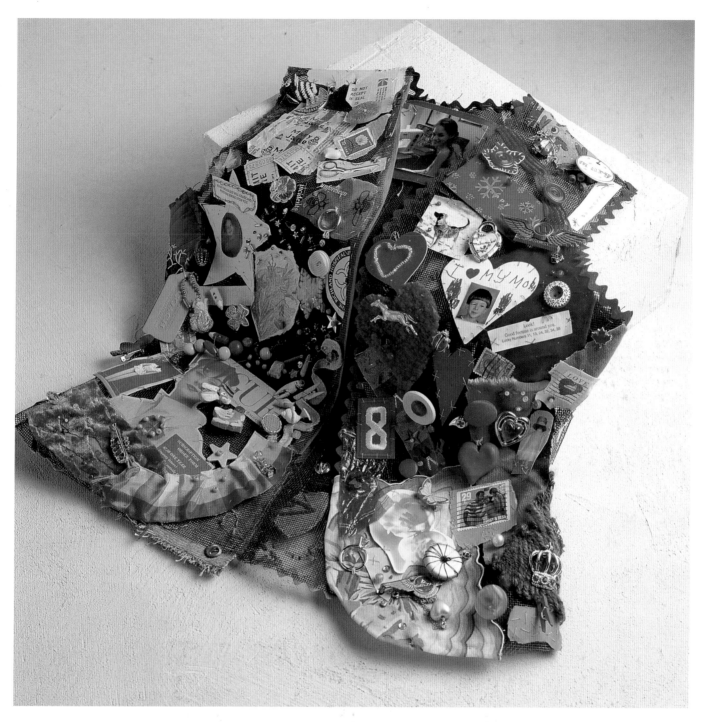

Tips: To attach photos and papers, punch a series of two holes placed side by side around the border of each with the sewing needle. Use a cross-stitch sewn through these holes to sew the paper to the screen.

To attach small objects, sew several strands of thread around the front of the object (so that it appears to be wrapped) as you push the needle from the front to the back of the screen.

Button & Paper Collage

MATERIALS AND TOOLS

Collection of buttons

Batiked and marbled papers or other colorful, printed papers

Large sheet of heavy black paper

Sewing machine with thread

Needle and thread

White craft glue

Small glass beads

Foamboard

Designer
Billi R. S. Rothove

THIS COLLAGE HAS SPECIAL MEANING to the designer because it links her symbolically to generations of women in her family who used the needle arts to make beautiful and useful items. Because so many of the buttons held special significance for her, she made a button map to record where she had placed each button and to whom it belonged. The collage—with its history of buttons—will be passed down as a family keepsake.

PROCESS

Cut out pieces of batiked and marbled papers, and arrange them in a patchwork pattern on a large sheet of black paper. Remove papers that fit together to form a quadrant of the design, and sew them together along the edges in a patchwork fashion with a zigzag stitch. (You can work with any size section of your choice; the point is to sew together smaller sections at a time.) Sew the papers for all of the quadrants together. Arrange and sew buttons to the patchwork quadrant by hand. Don't clip the thread when you're finished, but allow it to hang down loosely as part of the design. If you're using especially heavy buttons, glue them onto the piece before using thread. Add short strands of beads to the centers of some of the buttons by threading them and then attaching them through the buttonholes.

Arrange the paper pieces on the black paper in your original configuration. Tack the papers into place on the black paper with small dots of glue. Use a sewing machine threaded with black thread to overstitch the outside and inside edges of the quadrants with a zigzag stitch, so that the sections are neatly attached to the black paper.

Mount the piece on foamboad, and frame it as you wish.

This collage was inspired by accident. As I was searching through a jar full of old buttons, I recalled fond moments from my childhood: Twiddling great-grandma's Sunday dress button while she held me on her lap; leaning close to study a beautiful button while I learned French children's songs; listening to stories of adventurous travel. As I looked through the jar, I selected buttons that once belonged to the influential women in my life—great-grandmothers, grandmothers, and my mother. I added buttons from my own long-forgotten shirts and dresses.

At my studio table, I began arranging scraps of batiked and marbled papers made by myself and my mother, selecting those that enhanced the colors and magic I found in each of the family buttons.

To make your own button collage, you can also use old magazine pictures, greeting cards, gift wrap, or any paper or fabric with a pattern or meaningful picture as a colorful background.

—Billi R. S. Rothove

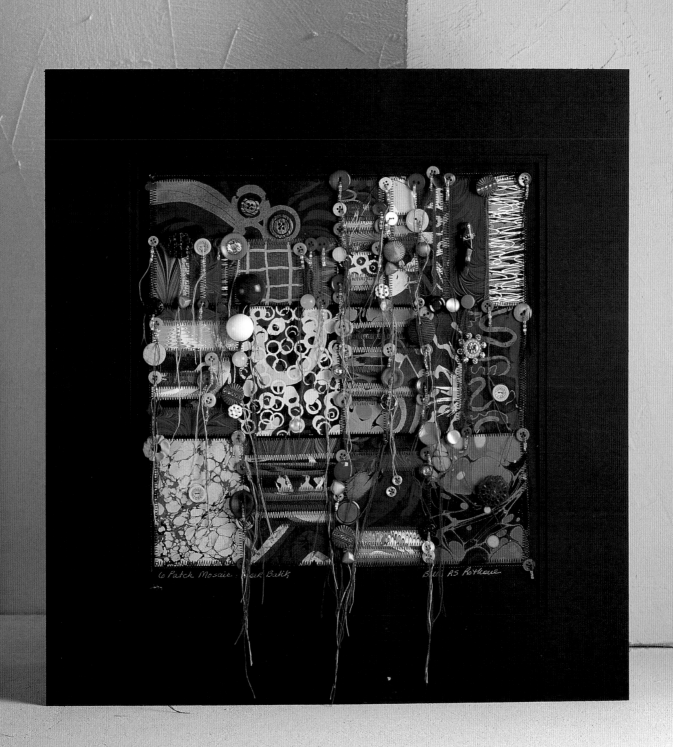

6 Patch Mosaic — Laser Batik   Buttons RS Rothous

Tissue Paper Ornaments

MATERIALS AND TOOLS

Large glass Christmas ornaments

Sheets of pastel-colored tissue paper

Patterned tissue papers (optional)

Watercolor paints

White craft glue

Paintbrush

Texturizing paint

Gift wrap, magazines, or other source of cutout images (optional)

Small piece of foamboard (optional)

Mat knife (optional)

Construction paper (optional)

Designer
Pei Ling Becker

LAYERS OF COLORED TISSUE PAPER and some added surface finishes turn simple Christmas ornaments into shimmering balls of pattern and color.

PROCESS

Paint glue onto a section of one of the ornaments in preparation for applying collaged paper. Tear sheets of tissue paper into strips. Paint several strips with different colors of watercolor paint, then press them in layers onto the ball. Don't worry about the colors bleeding into one another, but rather, allow this to happen. Use your fingers to continue to press and mold the papers onto the surface of the ball. Allow the tissue paper layer to dry.

Leave the ball as it is, or add cutout sections of decorative gift wrap or magazine illustrations to the surface. To raise cutouts off of the surface of the ball, cut out small squares of foamboard with a mat knife, and glue them into place on the surface of the ball. Glue small shapes or cutouts from magazines onto the raised squares to make them appear as if they are floating above the collage. If you want to add a fringe of leaves around the top of the ball, cut them out of construction paper and enhance them with lines of texturizing paint. Glue them into place around the top of the ball.

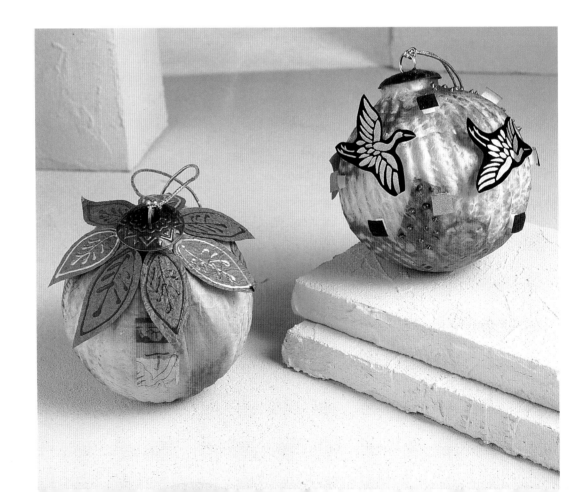

Confectionary Tray

THIS SWEET TREAT TRAY WAS CREATED BY THE DESIGNER as a gift for Mother's Day. She added handwritten phrases to the collage as a personal touch before sealing it with varnish.

PROCESS

Assemble a collection of papers, stickers, and other components with a confectionary theme. Tear the papers into pieces that emphasize the images you want to use in the collage.

Apply acrylic medium with the sponge brush or paintbrush to a portion of the tray. Begin pressing papers into place, overlapping them as you go. Paint more medium over the papers to adhere them to one another.

Create a random background with the components. To add visual organization to the design, place a few key elements in the foreground in a symmetrical arrangement around the edges of the tray (such as the cups and saucers that you see on this tray). Add highlights of gold leaf and gold thread and ribbon.

Allow the tray to dry. Spray it in a well-ventilated room or outside with a coat of matte lacquer spray, or paint it with another coat of acrylic medium to seal the surface.

MATERIALS AND TOOLS

Plastic serving tray

Tea bag wrappers

Tissue paper and gift wrap with Victorian print

Stickers with confection theme: tea cups, candy dishes, truffles, cupcakes, strawberries

Old postcards

Gold thread and ribbon

Gold leaf

Acrylic matte medium

Sponge brush or paintbrush

Matte lacquer spray (optional)

Designer
Diane Peterson

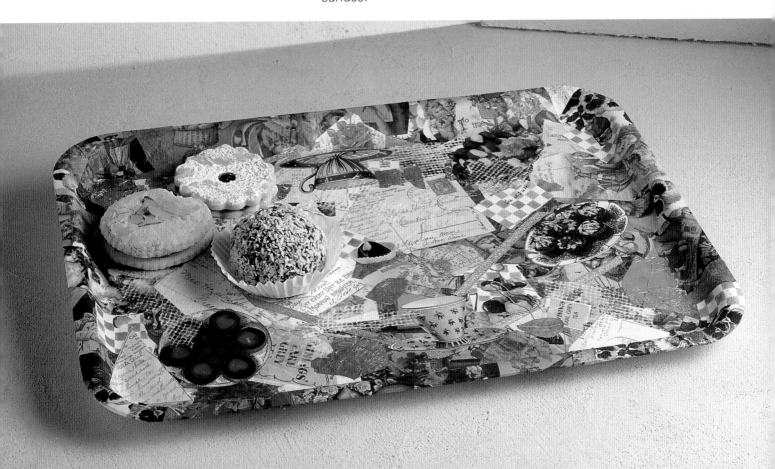

Easter Eggs

MATERIALS AND TOOLS

Uncooked eggs

Sewing needle

Colored scraps of magazine pages and newspapers

Acrylic gloss medium

Small plastic cup

Paintbrush

Wax paper

Designer
Maggie D. Jones

Use colorful scraps of paper from magazines and black and white papers from newspapers to transform eggshells into collaged forms. The designer has collected Easter eggs for years while adding her own dyed, painted, carved, and batiked eggs to her collection.

When she was asked to cover something unusual with collage, she couldn't resist trying it on an egg! Since she wanted to achieve a textural surface, she used thicker papers from magazines. If you want to make a smooth surface, try layering very small pieces of thin paper such as tissue paper instead.

PROCESS

Carefully pierce a hole in each end of an uncooked egg. Hold the egg up to your lips over a sink, and blow until the yolk and white of the egg run out. Turn on tap water, and place the egg underneath it until the water runs clear. Repeat this process with as many eggs as you'd like to collage.

Tear out colored images from magazines and newspapers. Sort your paper swatches into piles by hue. Tear the images into small pieces. Pour about 2 tablespoons (30 mL) of acrylic medium into the plastic cup, and add a small amount of water as a thinner.

Brush a small amount of medium onto the surface of one of the eggshells. Press a piece of paper into place on the shell, and immediately paint over the paper to help adhere it to the curved surface. Skim over the surface of the paper with your fingertips to smooth out any air bubbles. Continue to layer pieces of colored paper in this fashion until the surface is covered.

Place the egg on a piece of wax paper on a flat surface to dry. When the eggshell is dry, coat it with a layer of undiluted acrylic gloss medium.

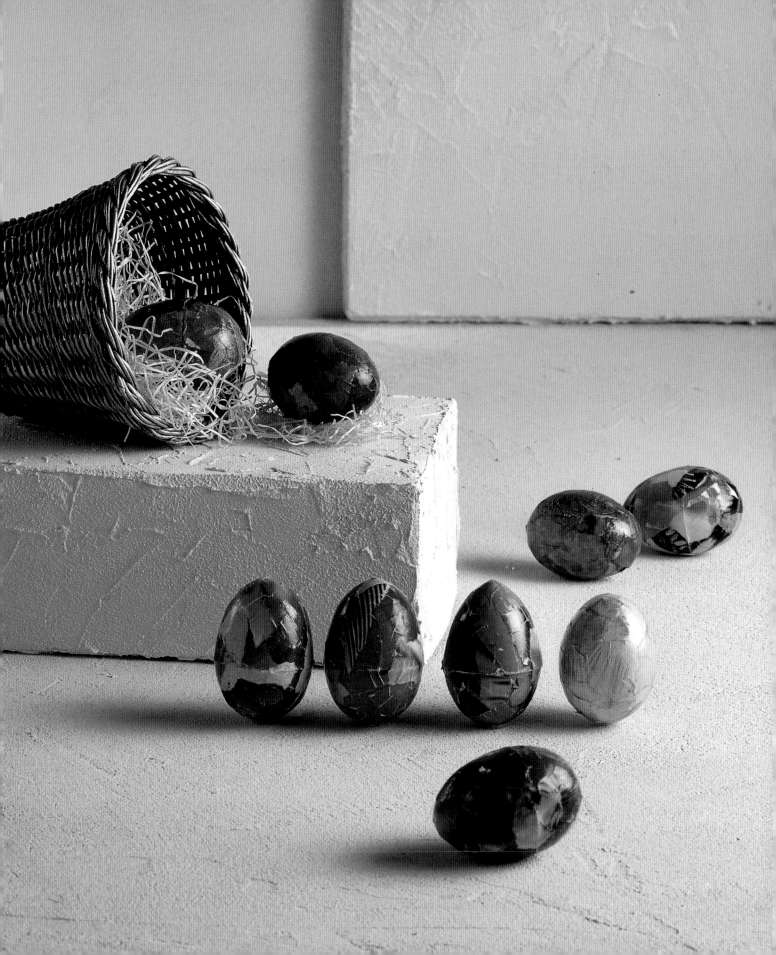

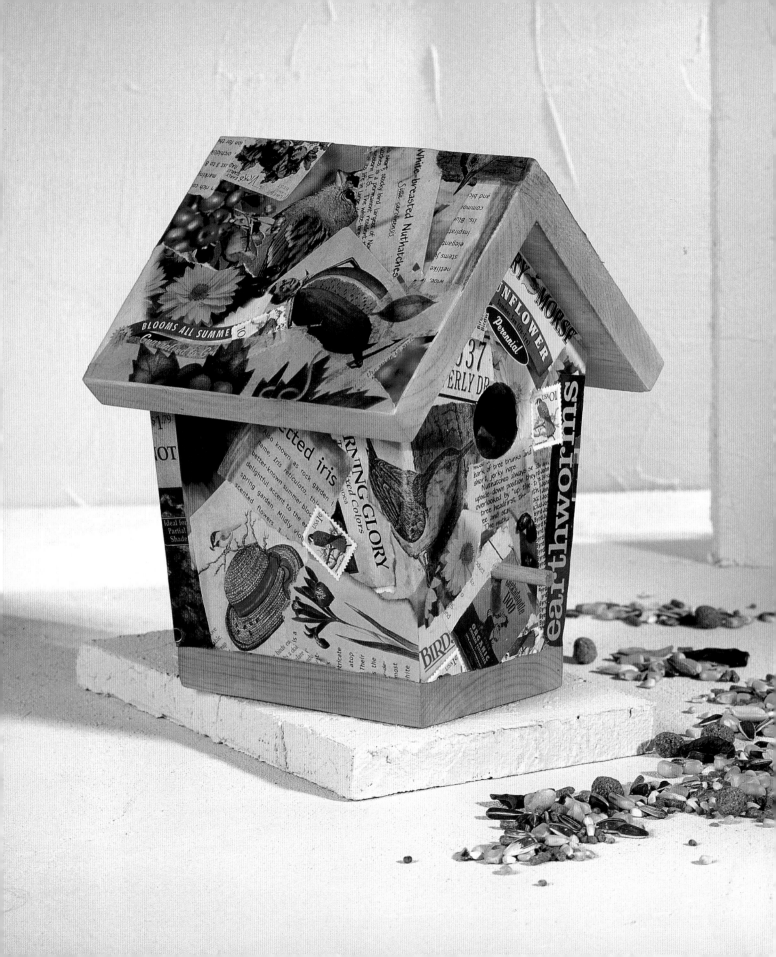

Collaged Birdhouse

THIS DESIGNER FOUND A PERFECT USE FOR a stack of beautifully printed seed packets saved over the years from her gardening adventures. She added other bird-related papers and created a handsome shelter for her backyard friends.

PROCESS

Collect seed packets, garden-related pictures from magazines and catalogues, and other printed papers with a gardening or bird theme.

Tear the packets and other printed materials into small pieces that highlight the images that are of interest for your collage. Use the sponge brush to coat a portion of the surface of the birdhouse with acrylic matte medium, and begin pressing the collage components into place, overlapping them as you go. Continue to add papers until you've covered the birdhouse.

Sponge brown wood stain randomly over certain portions of the collaged surface to lend it an antique look. Remove excess stain with a clean cloth. Add a few sunflower seeds to the still-wet surface, and allow the birdhouse to dry. Spray the birdhouse outside or in a well-ventilated room with matte lacquer spray or water sealant to waterproof it.

MATERIALS AND TOOLS

Unfinished wooden birdhouse

Empty seed packets

Seed and gardening catalogues

Canceled postage stamps

Phone book pages

Tissue paper printed with fruit pattern

Reproductions of antique vegetable labels

Dried, pressed leaves

Sunflower seeds

Acrylic matte medium

Brown wood stain (water- or oil-based)

Sponge brushes

Clean cloth

Matte lacquer spray or spray water sealant

Designer
Diane Peterson

Nostalgic Frame

MATERIALS AND TOOLS

Flat wooden frame

Acrylic paint in color of your choice

Paintbrush

Photocopied design motifs of your choice from copyright-free design book, gift wrap, wallpaper samples, or other source

Pencil

Scissors

Colored tissue paper

Acrylic matte medium

Blender pen (a pen that contains solvent for transferring)

Flat wooden spoon

Designer
Terry Taylor

WITH A FEW SIMPLE BUT WELL-PLACED design elements, this artist shows how simple it is to resuscitate an old frame or enhance a new one to make a thing of beauty.

PROCESS

Paint the frame with at least two coats of acrylic paint to serve as a background for your design. Allow the frame to dry between coats.

Select two or three simple design motifs that you want to overlap in two of the corners of your frame. (If you find a large design that you like, remember that you can cut out a portion of it, and enlarge it to fit your purposes.)

Decide which images you want to place on the frame first as the background pieces. Use a photocopy machine to enlarge or reduce these motifs to fit the corners of the frame.

Place your photocopy facedown, and use a pencil to outline the motifs on the back of the paper. Cut out the shapes with scissors so that they can serve as templates. (These shapes will be the reverse of your photocopies.) Use these templates to cut out reverse shapes from sheets of tissue paper.

Use acrylic matte medium and a paintbrush to affix the tissue shapes to the frame. Allow the frame to dry overnight. Use a blender pen containing solvent and a wooden spoon to transfer the original photocopied motifs that you cut out onto the tissue paper. Rub the pen across the back of the photocopied designs, and then burnish, or rub, the back of the paper with a flat wooden spoon.

Affix the other cutout motifs on top of the tissue paper motifs. Allow the frame to dry. Paint one to two coats of varnish over the entire frame to seal it.

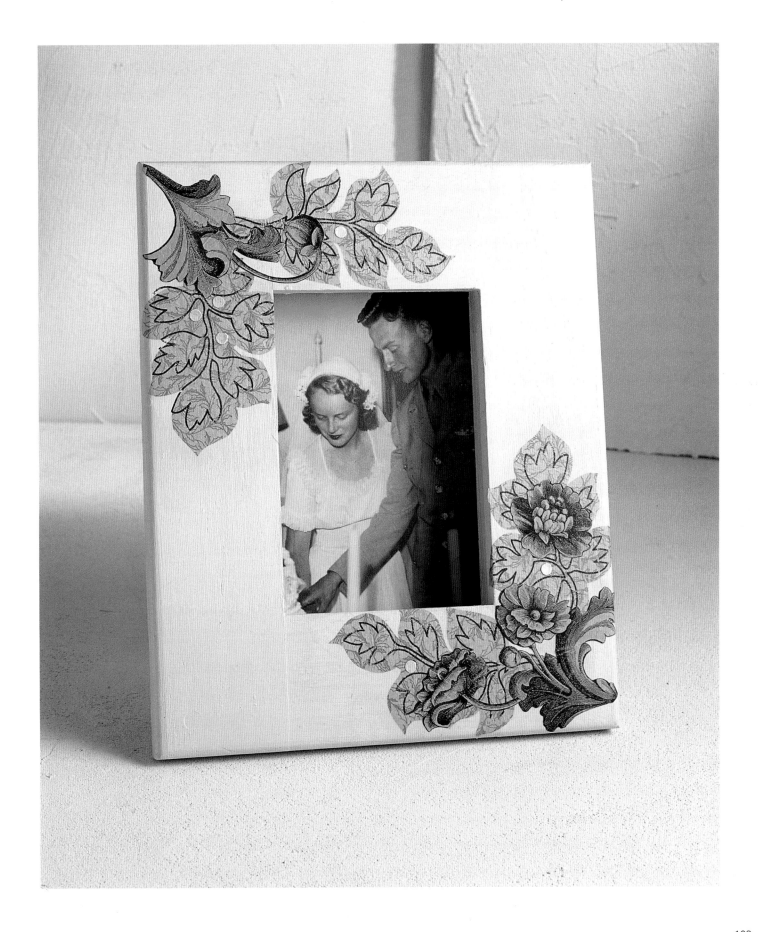

Birthday Box

**MATERIALS
AND TOOLS**

Paper gift box

Gift wrapping papers
and tissue paper

Ribbons

Acrylic gloss medium

Small plastic cup

Paintbrush

*Designer
Maggie D. Jones*

WHEN THIS DESIGNER CELEBRATED A MILESTONE BIRTHDAY, she was honored with a surprise birthday party. She contemplated what to do with all of the personal cards that were written to her, as well as the beautiful wrappings and ribbons. She decided to create a collaged "time capsule" for her accumulations from one of the gift boxes.

PROCESS

To make your own birthday box, save the wrappings, ribbons, cards, and a box that you like from a birthday party. Tear the papers into small pieces.

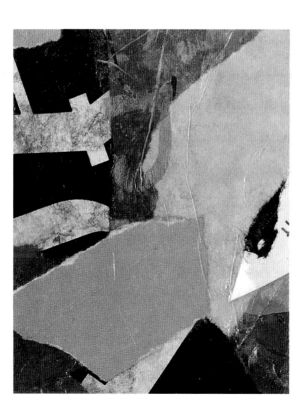

Dilute the acrylic medium with a small amount of water in the plastic cup. Apply a coat of the acrylic medium with a brush to the surface of your box. Allow it to dry to seal the surface. Apply more medium to the surface, and place the torn pieces on the box in a design that you like. Overlap and layer them as you go.

When you've finished covering the top and sides of your box, apply a full strength coat of acrylic medium to create a shine on the surface and preserve your treasures. Place cards, extra ribbons, photos, and party decorations that you'd like to save inside the box for safekeeping.

Note: You can opt to use the dry adhesive method described on pages 22 through 24 to apply the collage components.

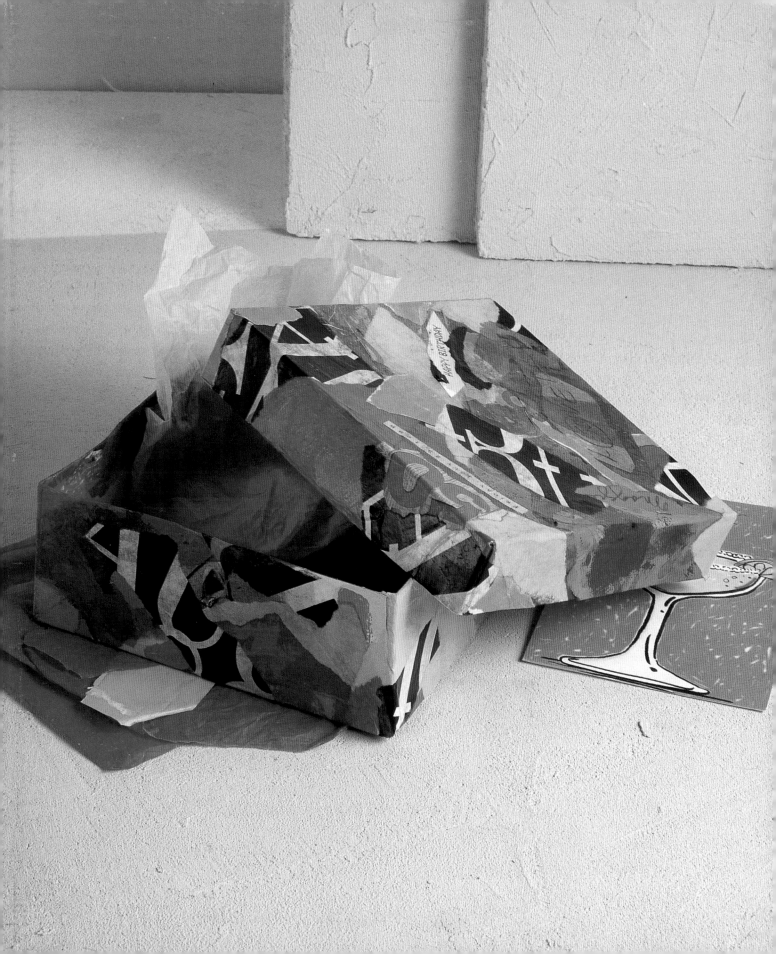

INDEX

SUPPLIERS

For Release Paper, Acrylic Image Transfer Paper, and Tacking Irons:

Talbot Arts
7 Amity Rd.
Warwick, NY 10990
1-800-375-5133
Art Media
902 S.W. Yamhill St.
Portland, OR 97205
1-503-223-3724

Fascinating Folds
P.O. Box 10070
Glendale, AZ
1-800-968-2418
www.fascinating-folds.com

For Release Paper:
Light Impressions
P.O. Box 22708
Rochester, NY 14692
1-800-828-6216

DESIGNERS

Kathleen M. Anderson is a surface designer who lives in Kent, WA, with her husband of 34 years. **Pei Ling Becker** is a nationally known artist who lives in Black Mountain, NC. **Tana Boerger** is an entrepreneur and classically trained artist who lives in Washington, DC. **Carolyn Brooks** is an artist and art therapist who lives in Asheville, NC. **Amy Cook** is an artist and writer who lives in San Francisco, CA. **Mary D'Alton** of Spring Green, WI, is an artist, photostylist, author, and propmaker. **Dayle Doroshaw** of Ft. Bragg, CA, is a polymer clay artist and owner of a design studio. **Barbara Evans** of Ventura, CA, has worked as a designer for craft magazines for 20 years. **Maggie D. Jones** of Greenville, SC, is an artist, photographer, and teacher. **Rose Kelly** is a mixed media artist who lives in Oakland, CA. **Megan Kirby** is a graphic artist who lives in Asheville, NC. **Karen Page** is a mixed media artist who lives in Port Townsend, WA. **Jean Penland** is an artist, designer, and teacher who lives in Asheville, NC. **Diane Peterson** is a gourd artist who lives in Asheville, NC. **Billi R. S. Rothove** is a Tennessee fiber artist, has been creating images in fibers and needleart for 25 years. **Pat G. Samuels** is a studio textile artist who lives in the Blue Ridge Mountains of NC. **Cori Saraceni** is a metal and fiber artist who lives in Asheville, NC. **Kathryn Semolic** is a mixed media artist who owns Spider Mountain Studio in Burnet, TX. **Delda Skinner** is a published artist who lives in Austin, TX, who now specializes in bookmaking and book arts. **Terry Taylor** of Asheville, NC, is a mixed media artist. **Kim Tibbals-Thompson** of Waynesville, NC, is a graphic designer and artist. **Luann Udell** is a mixed media artist who lives in Keene, NH. **Lynn Whipple** of Winter Park, FL, is a mixed media artist who exhibits nationally. **Nancy Worrell** is a published author and artist who lives in Chapel Hill, NC. **Ellen Zahorec** is a mixed media artist who now lives in Cincinatti, OH.